MISSIONS
AND
MISSIONARIES
IN THE PACIFIC

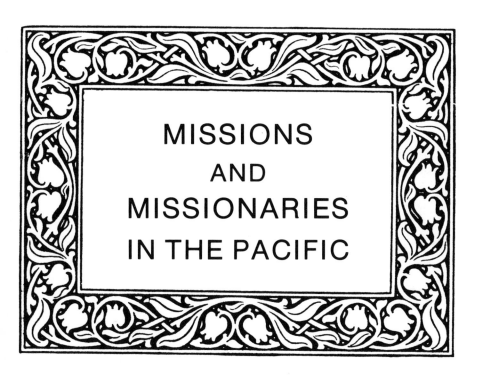

MISSIONS
AND
MISSIONARIES
IN THE PACIFIC

Edited by
Char Miller

Symposium Series
Volume 14

The Edwin Mellen Press
New York and Toronto

Library of Congress Cataloging in Publication Data
Main entry under title:

Missions and missionaries in the Pacific.

(Symposium series ; v. 14)
Bibliography: p.
1. Missions--Islands of the Pacific--Addresses,
essays, lectures. 2. Islands of the Pacific--Church
history--Addresses, essays, lectures. I. Miller,
Char. II. Title. III. Series: Symposium series
(Edwin Mellen Press) ; v. 14.
BV3670.M53 1985   266'.0099   85-5074
ISBN 0-88946-705-6

Symposium Series
Series ISBN 0-88946-989-X

For information contact:
The Edwin Mellen Press
P.O. Box 450
Lewiston, New York 14092

Printed in the United States of America

CONTRIBUTORS

James A. Boutilier is Associate Professor of History and Head of the History and Political Economy Departments at Royal Roads Military College (Canada). He is editor of *Mission, Church and Sect in Oceania* (1978) and author of many articles on the missionary experience.

Charles W. Forman, D. Willis James Professor of Mission at Yale Divinity School, is author of *The Island Churches of the South Pacific: Emergence in the Twentieth Century* (1982) and was recently president of the American Society of Missiology.

Char Miller, Assistant Professor of History at Trinity University (Texas), is author of *Fathers and Sons: The Bingham Family and the American Mission* (1982) and currently serves as Chair of the Executive Committee of the Pacific Studies Association.

TABLE OF CONTENTS

INTRODUCTION

CHAR MILLER

The focus of mission history has altered over time. No longer is it seen simply as a chronicle of the battle between Christianity and heathenism, between the forces of light and dark, visions that imbued 19th Century missionary self-evaluations. Rather, as H.E. Maude recently observed, the study of missions has "progressed from the level of apologetics and works intended for the edification of adherents to that of objective historiography." That objectivity now characterizes mission scholarship does not mean, however, that that scholarship has reached a plateau, that little more can be expected from its practitioners. On the contrary, the field has undergone periodic transformations. Fifteen years ago, for instance, the Journal de la Sociétié des Océanists published a massive volume of then current scholarship on missions, as well as reams of statistical data and archival material that cast much light on missionary activity; the field, in a sense, was becoming professionalized. A decade later that professionalism emerged full blown in Mission, Church and Sect in Oceania, a monograph sponsored by the Association for Social Anthropology in Oceania, one that revealed the exciting and sophisticated findings that cross-cultural research and interdisciplinary perspectives could produce. But even that was not enough, for, in his introductory essay to Mission, Church and Sect, Kenelm Burridge sensed a "growing consciousness among students of society and

to Mission, Church and Sect, Kenelm Burridge sensed a
"growing consciousness among students of society and
culture...that the missionary contribution both in action
and in reflective scholarship should be reevaluated" once
again. And, he predicted, that reevaluation would emerge
swiftly within the next decade, a prediction that reveals,
among other things, the rapidity with which scholarly
concerns evolve.[1]

Burridge's was also an accurate prediction: We now are
five years into that decade and the reevaluation seems to be
in full force. One need but peruse the rich bibliography
that the Journal of Pacific History publishes annually to
recognize how extensive that reassessment has become. It
includes revisions in the biographies of major missionaries,
extended analyses of missionary efforts generally, running
from case studies of particular churches in particular
locales to more sweeping accounts of the impact of
particular faiths in Oceania, to even more broadly conceived
discussions of all Island churches in the Pacific. These
efforts are ecumenical, addressing the Protestant and
Catholic experience, as well as international, chronicling
the perceptions of American, English, French and German
missionaries operating in the region.[2]

This expanded coverage is only a partial reflection of
the ways that the study of missions has widened in scope and
deepened in analytical power: The approach scholars now
take to the study of missionization itself has undergone
fundamental alterations. Increasingly, historians and
others emphasize the need for a sensitive awareness to and a
sophisticated reconstruction of the context of missionary
labors, an approach that operates on a number of levels.
One of these is a heightened understanding of the world that
spawned the foreign missionaries who came to the Pacific, of
the social and intellectual realm in which they moved and of

the ideas and beliefs--the cultural baggage--they carried with them. Without a close look at such issues there would remain the possibility of making the same mistake that earlier commentators made when they tarred the missionaries with the brush of "Puritanism" and left it at that. Since the missionaries took themselves and their work seriously, so should scholars if they wish to understand, even to recapture the lives of those who brought Christianity to Oceania.[3]

They must do so for another reason as well: The missionaries' national origins and cultural values are a vital element in what Francis Hezel has recently reiterated as the critical issue confronting Pacific historians-- contact between cultures. And clearly missionary activities offer a rich opportunity to explore the varied dimensions of cultural contact, an obvious one of which involves the missionaries themselves--how they perceived the particular island culture in which they were immersed, how that perception shaped their behavior and, in specific, their conversion efforts, and, to what degree, if any, were they able to realign island life to meet their standards of a godly life. These issues are well documented in the missionaries' voluminous public correspondence as well as in their private letters and diaries, issues that have played a large role in the scholarly literature on missionization.[4]

The interactions of cultures, of course, are reciprocal. The missionaries' success in converting a particular population, for example, was rarely simply due to ministerial effort or to the blessings of Christianity. Of prime importance in the exchange of religion was the indigenous people's _desire_ to convert, desires that often had more to do with internal island politics than with the persuasiveness of a missionary; he or she was persuasive because the particular islanders wished to be persuaded.

Hawaii is but a case in point. There, the nobility--or at
least portions of it--were attracted to the New England
evangelists because an alliance with them seemed an
effective way to legitimize the power and position of those
who, as Barrere and Sahlins argue, "could not claim the
traditional sanctions of rule."[5]

Political stature was not the only benefit Hawaiians (or
other Pacific Islanders) gained when they allied with the
missionaries. Instruction in the foreigners' language, in
English or French or German, could also provide the people--
perhaps the leadership especially--with the ability to carry
on trade with the outside world, to accumulate western
consumer goods and weapons, all of which perforce enhanced
one's domestic standing. Conversion to Christianity, in
short, could be but a means to an end. To understand that
end it is therefore important to explore Island history and
culture for a fuller sense of the context in which cultural
contact occurred, of how and why the islanders reacted to
Christianity as they did. The study of missions, then, is
also but a means to an end, one that can facilitate a
broader understanding of the complexity of Pacific history.

The three essays presented in **Missions and Missionaries
in the Pacific** reveal, if nothing else, how complex mission
and Pacific history can be. Originally delivered to the
first annual meeting of the Pacific Studies Association held
in San Francisco in late December 1983, and revised since
that time, the essays approach the problem of mission
history from diverse angles. James A. Boutilier, in "We
Fear Not For The Ultimate Triumph," examines the processes
of conversion, and seeks to isolate and describe "those
variables that seemed to have determined the success or
failure of the conversion phase" in the 19th Century South

Pacific.

The variables were many, perhaps as many as there were
missionaries operating in the South Pacific. In particular,
however, Boutilier stresses that one key to conversion lay
with   indigenous   politics   and,   relatedly,   with   the
receptivity of Oceanic cultures to imported value systems
that either held values in common with Island beliefs (such
as tapus) or which could be used to sustain traditional
hierarchies or to legitimize challengers' positions.   In
addition,   he   finds   that   beachcombers   and   other   non-
missionary Europeans also played important roles in the
conversion process (though perhaps unknowingly), for when
these   men   challenged   traditional   social   constructs   or
ignored tapus (and emerged unscathed) their actions
undermined the force of social prescription and increased
the chances that Islanders might accept Christianity. And,
of course, there was an array of variables that concerned
the missionaries themselves: From their personalities,
values and physical health to their access to western goods
for   exchange   with   the   Islanders;   from   the   damaging
internicine struggles between competing Christian missions
to a mission's ability to call in its nation's warships to
resolve Island disputes and thereby strengthen its position.

In isolating these and other variables, Boutilier also
probes   that   series   of   difficult--perhaps   ultimately
unanswerable--questions: When did the missionary message
supplant the "traditional spiritual system," when could
success be named and how was it defined? These questions,
in truth, thematically link the three essays in this volume,
for together they reveal that the definition of success
differed among missionaries and between faiths;   the
Catholics and Protestants, for instance, who rarely agreed
on anything, used different criteria to measure the success
of the respective missionary empires. Nor do these essays

suggest that these measurements remained static; rather they
changed over time, reflecting new circumstances or altered
tactics. The Protestant missionaries to Hawaii believed
early on that success not only depended on the number and
sincerity of religious conversions but on the effect that
the missionaries had on the Hawaiian landscape itself; when
the mission's agricultural experiments failed, and its
"agriculturalist" returned to the United States, the mission
modified its visions of what constituted success. That kind
of flexibility emerged as well when the London Missionary
Society and the American Board of Commissioners for Foreign
Missions (ABCFM) began to rely heavily on Island converts
rather than on westerners to spread the Christian message.
And full devolution of control of religious life, the
emergence of independent and self-sufficient Island
churches, may mark, Charles Forman argues, the final sign of
success. In the end, however, the definition of success is
as elusive as its timing is difficult to pinpoint. But what
is clear, Boutilier reminds us, is that the missionaries
"were only one set of players in [the] much larger drama" of
conversion and that it "was the islanders who determined the
success or failure of missionary endeavors."

     "Domesticity Abroad: Work and Family in the Sandwich
Island Mission," Char Miller's contribution to the
symposium, plays off a point that Boutilier raises in
connection with the efficacy of missionary endeavors--their
success, he observes, was to a considerable degree shaped by
internal factors, those concerned with the missionary's
physical and psychological health, with their sense of
themselves and their mission, and the impact that these had
on their work outside the mission compound.

     The impact was considerable in the case of the
missionaries to Hawaii. Their official task, of course, was
to promulgate Christianity and to rid the Islands of

"heathenism." That task was complicated, however, by an ideological constraint, one that deeply influenced and occasionally transformed the manner in which they labored. The ABCFM, the sponsoring body of the Sandwich Island Mission, believed that Christian families would be more effective than individual missionaries, than bachelors, in spreading Christ's message, a belief based on the Board's perception of the fundamental role the nuclear family played in western civilization; if Hawaii (and the rest of the world) was to be remolded in the image of America, then American families (consisting of husband, wife and children) should serve as role models; when the first American mission sailed to the Pacific in 1820, it comprised seven married couples.

This strategy, which inextricably linked mission work and family life, had its benefits. The missionaries (male and female) believed that the American women's presence favorably impressed the Islanders, enabled them to visit and proselytize in arenas in which the men of the mission were less effective, thereby increasing the mission's chances for success. But this tight connection between work and family also had its costs, costs largely incurred by the women of the mission. Their public roles as missionaries, for instance, clashed with their private ones as mothers and helpmates, as symbols of American domesticity. And over time, especially with the births of their children, the women began to withdraw from active work outside the mission's walls. As these children matured, new concerns emerged; the question of how to raise mission children in the Islands sparked endless debate and much tension, and was usually resolved by sending the children back to the United States. These resolutions, both that of the women withdrawing from active work and of the children's departure not only engendered frustration on an individual level, but, in turn, diminished for a time the mission's overall effectiveness.

The 20th Century missionary experience in the Pacific differs from that of the preceding two centuries. 18th and 19th Century missionaries were pioneers of much certitude and conviction, traits that helped expand the Protestant denominations and Catholic orders' spheres of influence throughout Oceania. For these early missionaries, the numbers of converts were, among other things, a sign of that expansion and an indication of its success. These heady times and exciting folk, naturally enough, have drawn much greater scholarly attention than have those who labored in the 20th Century, when consolidation rather than conquest has seemed to characterize missionary activities.

But there is an exciting component to the history of 20th Century mission work--devolution of control from metropolitan ecclesiastical centers to local congregations or national churches. This complex process, which in some places began as early as the 19th Century, but which really emerged as a powerful force in Pacific mission history in the post-World War II era, and thus runs parallel to political independence in the Pacific, has not been clear-cut. Many difficulties and complications have arisen in the Islands' Churches' quest for independence, a struggle that Charles Forman chronicles in "Playing Catch-Up Ball: A History of Financial Independence in the Pacific Island Churches."

The pattern of financial affairs of Island Churches has differed from denomination to denomination, Forman argues. Those denominations that expected that the local village missions would be self-supporting, that their reliance upon outside funding would be minimal or at least would decrease as part of the natural course of events, generally set a pattern that would, in time, be duplicated on the national level; examples of these, Forman notes, are the missions that the ABCFM and its British counterpart, the London Missionary Society, commenced and which gained independence over time. The Catholic missions, on the other hand, had no expectation of self-sufficiency, relied heavily upon funding from European sources, and thus did not encourage "the people [to] feel that the continuing support of the church was their responsibility," a situation that encouraged continued dependence. Despite these differences, however, all Christian missions introduced higher levels of spending than the indigenous forms of worship had entailed, as the missions expanded into higher levels of education, centralized administration and supported missionary ships and salaries. Although many of these burdens were overcome by the mid-20th Century when these churches achieved independence, that independence (ecclesiastical and financial) did not by itself resolve the Island Churches' problems. Rather, new forms of dependence emerged. Western Pacific churches, for example, underwrote educational and medical services in the newly-independent nations, for which they were forced to turn to outside donors. And most recently, the Pacific churches have found that their part in the worldwide ecumenical movement--embodied in the Pacific Conference of Churches--has entailed new costs and continued dependency. Despite these costs, the churches of the Pacific are generally in solid financial shape, but, Forman concludes, they must still adjust themselves to "the interests and priorities of outsiders." Independence, in short, is not yet won.

These three essays, which draw upon difference sources and probe a variety of issues over a broad period of time, reflect, we hope, the breadth, depth and continuing vitality of mission history. Although none is definitive--all are clearly exploratory in nature--we nonetheless hope, too, that each contributes to a better understanding of the complex processes involved in missionary activities, that each presents a challenge to further research, one that will perforce enhance our knowledge of some of the historical forces at work in the Pacific.[6]

The authors of this slim volume have compiled a large number of debts, and I would like to acknowledge and thank all who made the conference and the subsequent publication possible. The American Historical Association generously provided the Pacific Studies Association with a conference room during its 1983 annual meeting. Those who participated in the symposium on Missions and Missionaries in the Pacific not only traveled a great distance to do so, coming from as far away as Hawaii and Connecticut, Canada and Oklahoma, but gave much needed and constructive criticism of the papers presented. A special thanks is due Sharon Tiffany, who read James Boutilier's essay with great care and to Judith Lipsett who read the entire manuscript with a sharp editorial eye. Char Miller's research was underwritten by a Trinity University Faculty Development Committee Grant (1982) for which he is grateful. Most of all, however, I am greatly indebted to Margaret Morrissey and Kathy Zuehl, secretaries of the History Department of Trinity University, and to Lisa Bruening, Jennifer Jenks and David Robertson for their capable typing of the manuscript; their friendship, support and laughter have made this project a pleasure indeed. Finally, this volume is dedicated to Benjamin, who has shown me the joys of parenthood and from whom I have learned much about the complex interaction between work and family.

San Antonio, Texas
1984

NOTES

[1] *Journal de La Société des Océanistes*, 25, December 1969; Kenelm Burridge, "Introduction: Missionary Occasions," in James A. Boutilier, Daniel T. Hughes and Sharon W. Tiffany, eds., *Mission, Church, and Sect in Oceania*, [Ann Arbor: University of Michigan Press, 1978], p.1.

[2] See for example, David Hilliard, *God's Gentlemen: A History of the Melanesian Mission, 1849-1942*, [St. Lucia: University of Queensland Press, 1978]; Ralph Witgen, *The Founding of the Roman Catholic Church in Oceania 1825 to 1859*, [Canberra: Australian National University Press, 1979]; Neil Gunson, *Messengers of Grace: Evangelical Missionaries in the South Seas,1797-1860*. [Oxford: Oxford University Press, 1978]; John Garrett, *To Live Among the Stars: Christian Origins in Oceania* [Geneva: World Council of Churches, 1982]; Charles Foreman, *The Island Churches of the South Pacific: Emergence in the Twentieth Century*, [Maryknoll: Orbis Books, 1982].

[3] Neil Gunson, *Messengers of Grace* is a good place to start for social and intellectual background of some of the missionary movements. Gunson's approach is an effective contrast to that of Louis B. Wright and Mary Fry, *Puritans in the South Seas* [New York: Holt and Co., 1936].

[4] Francis Hezel, *The First Taint of Civilization* [Honolulu: University of Hawaii Press, 1983].

[5] Dorothy Barrere and Marshall Sahlins, "Tahitians in the early history of Hawaiian Christianity: The Journal of Toketa," *Hawaiian Journal of History*, 13, 1979, p. 24.

[6] "Domesticity Abroad," for example, was completed when Patricia Grimsham's seminal essay, "Christian Woman, Pious Wife, Faithful Mother, Devoted Missionary: Conflicts in Roles of American Missionary Women in Nineteenth Century Hawaii," appeared in *Feminist Studies*, Fall 1983. The two essays complement each other in many respects, especially regarding some of the internal strains that emerged in the Sandwich Island Mission. However, their historiographical foci differ: Grimshaw is concerned with women's work; mine centers on family dynamics, on the complex interaction of women, men and children--these actors, and the Hawaiians themselves, brought into sharp focus the critical concerns of work and family.

JAMES A. BOUTILIER

WE FEAR NOT THE ULTIMATE TRIUMPH:

FACTORS EFFECTING THE CONVERSION PHASE OF

NINETEENTH-CENTURY MISSIONARY ENTERPRISES

INTRODUCTION

The nineteenth century was a period of major missionary activity in the South Pacific. The first European missionaries--members of the London Missionary Society (LMS) --arrived in Tahiti in 1797 and during the next one hundred years they and their successors pushed the Christian frontier westward to New Guinea. In the words of John Williams, the leader of the LMS expedition to Samoa in 1830, the missionary enterprise was "incomparably the most effective machinery" created to advance the moral and spiritual interests of mankind.[2] While nineteenth-century missionaries were pleased to attribute the outcome of their labors to divine intervention, I am obliged to argue -- in order to prevent my paper from ending here -- that God's hand was not sufficient to explain why some missionary enterprises failed while others enabled their authors to snatch "victory out of imminent defeat."[3] My intention, therefore, is to isolate those variables that appear to have determined the success or failure of the conversion phase of those labors.

The principal variables may be summarized briefly. Missionaries were important agents of change. Their presence, their perceived association with great natural and supernatural powers, their possession of and access to material goods, their esoteric knowledge, and their activities, threatened the spiritual and political status quo in the islands. They assisted in the destruction of the old order and the erection of a cosmological framework to explain and legitimize the new order. Their attempts to change Oceanic cultures were resisted by traditional power brokers. Missionaries normally sought access to key actors whose patronage was seen to be vital to the success of the Christian endeavor. Their patrons (particularly in hierarchically-organized Polynesia), in turn, came to see that the new religion offered a convenient vehicle for working out old rivalries, for gaining material wealth, and for advancing political ambitions. Missionaries were themselves frequently at odds with other Europeans, many of whom had unwittingly set the stage for conversion. In other circumstances, missionaries found themselves pitted against "the wicked intrigues of Popery"[4] or Protestant heresy in inter- or intra-mission struggles that affected the outcome of mission labors. Often missionaries operated under conditions of grave danger, while death or disease brought their efforts to an end. In some cases warships came to their rescue, punishing the "savages" or exploiting the mission presence to advance imperial designs. Personalities, luck, linguistic ability, the metropolitan background of the mission, and the degree to which the Word--with all of the socio-political baggage attendant thereto--meshed with the value system of the host culture, all of these things influenced the success or failure of efforts at conversion.

I plan to examine these and other issues in this paper with reference to eight areas of missionary activity in Melanesia and Polynesia, exclusive of Hawaii: Tahiti (LMS), Tonga (Wesleyan and Marist), the Cooks (LMS), Samoa (LMS and Wesleyan), New Caledonia (Marist), the Gilbert and Ellice now Kiribati and Tubalu (LMS and American Board

Commissioners for Foreign Missions   ABCFM), the Solomons (Marist and Melanesian Mission), and New Guinea (LMS).

My focus is on conversion, rather than on consolidation. This raises the problem of determining satisfactorily when the conversion process becomes irreversible. The first baptism in Tonga, for example, took place in 1829 following three attempts, one by the LMS (1797-1800) and two by the Wesleyans (1822-1823 and 1826-), to establish a foothold there. That baptism did not mark the conversion of the Tongan people, but it did inaugurate a process which, despite setbacks, was destined to transform Tonga into a Christian kingdom.

In other cases, the "moment" of conversion, the moment when the imported message supplants the traditional spiritual system, is more difficult to pinpoint. Throughout the latter half of the nineteenth century the Melanesian Mission of the Church of England recruited young Solomon Islanders from Malaita for conversion and training in New Zealand and (after 1867) at Norfolk Island. There were no white Melanesian Mission missionaries serving on Malaita in the way that there were Wesleyans at work on Tongatapu. Instead, the Word was brought to Malaita by islander converts returning after their period of schooling. The conversion process on that island was extremely confused. Thousands of other Malaitans were repatriated during this period following labor service in Queensland. Some of them had been converted during their absence by the Queensland Kanaka Mission (QKM). They, no doubt, contributed in their own way to the conversion process. What is more, at the beginning of the twentieth century other missions, like the Roman Catholic Marists and the islands' version of the QKM, the South Sea Evangelical Mission, began to labor on Malaita. Thus it is extremely difficult to say, with reference to an island where there are still pagan enclaves,

by whom and when the conversion of the population was
assured.[6]

A note of caution is in order. The isolation of
individual elements or variables is attended with
difficulties. There is an old saying that you cannot make
an omelette without breaking eggs. What I have attempted to
do is to reverse the process--to run the movie backwards, as
it were--and isolate those variables (or eggs) which
determine the outcome of missionary endeavors. Those
endeavors --known in contemporary literature under the
portmanteau term "missionization"--involved a dialectical
interplay of culture, personalities, and events. Each
missionary encounter was unique. Yet, collectively, those
encounters shared much in common. In highlighting and
isolating those commonalities complex processes will be
subject to simplification and distortion.

THE "FUNERAL OF BIGOTRY"[7]

The LMS mission to Tahiti was a product of the
Evangelical Revival, a religious movement that swept Europe
and America in the second half of the eighteenth century.
The Revival, in turn, was a product of the Age of
Enlightenment during which a skeptical and egalitarian
spirit combined with nascent nationalism to topple the
citadels of the ancien regime in the American and French
Revolutions. Central to the Revival was the undertaking of
the Great Commission, the "conversion of the individual
through recognition of the gravity of sin, heartfelt
repentance, and trust in the self-sacrifice of Christ to
restore the believer to union with God."[8]

Two communities of non-conformists, the Calvinistic
Methodists and the Wesleyans, emerged from the Revival in
England. They differed fundamentally over the issue of
predestination. The Calvinists, grouped around George

Whitfield, argued that mankind was divided into two
irreconcilable groups: the elect, who were destined to
enjoy salvation, and the reprobate who were doomed to
damnation. This double predestination was anathema to John
Wesley's followers who maintained that Christ died to save
all men.

In 1795 Calvinistic Methodists and Anglicans formed the
Missionary Society, which came to be known after 1818 as the
LMS. Encouraged by the publication of Cook's and Bligh's
voyages to Tahiti, the LMS selected that island as the
location for their first mission.[9] However, differences of
opinion surfaced during the voyage of the mission ship Duff
to the Pacific, and when the party arrived in Polynesia it
split up--the larger group staying in Tahiti, while smaller
groups moved to the Marquesas and Tonga. The Tongan mission
was short-lived; caught up in a civil war, the missionaries
opted (save for one who "went native") to retire to New
South Wales.[10]

The LMS succeeded in converting Tahiti by 1815, but the
islands to the west still lay in "darkness." It was
decided, therefore, to train Polynesian converts as mission
teachers and to dispatch them to neighboring archipelagos.
The first such teachers--two Society Islanders named Papeiha
and Vahapata--were delivered to the Cook Islands by John
Williams in 1821. By 1834 Rarotonga (the main island) was,
in Williams' words, "completely free of pagan idolatry."[11]

Meanwhile, the Wesleyans, who had established strong
roots in Australia and New Zealand, arrived in Tonga in
1826.[12] By 1833 the central and northern groups of Ha'a'ai
and Vava'u had gone over to the new religion. However, the
political and religious unification of the Friendly Islands
was not effected by the principal Wesleyan convert,
Taufa'ahau, until 1852.

One of the reasons for the delay was the arrival in
Tonga of members of the new French missionary order, the
Society of Mary, or Marists for short. Established in 1835,
the Marists, like the Wesleyans and LMS before them, were
products of their age. The authority of the Roman Catholic
church in France was severely undermined during the
Revolutionary and Napoleonic eras. However, the period of
reaction after the Battle of Waterloo saw the church regain
much of its power. But at the same time La Gloire began to
fade. French regimes became more work-a-day, and a self-
conscious desire developed to achieve renewed greatness
through foreign adventures. The church became a means to
that end. More than any of the other missions discussed in
this paper, the Marists and their companion French orders
became instruments of empire, aided and abetted by French
pro-consuls and gunboat captains.[13]

The Marists arrived in Tonga in October 1837.[14] Within
a week the Wesleyan missionaries, Thomas and Brooks, had
obliged them to leave. But they were back again in June
1842, aligning themselves with the opponents of Taufa'ahau.

Taufa'ahau's successes encouraged the growth of
Wesleyanism in neighboring Samoa, where the LMS had
established a beachhead on Savai'i in 1830. In order to
avoid an unseemly struggle for converts, the Wesleyans and
LMS entered into a comity agreement that delimited their
respective spheres of influence. The Wesleyans were to
concentrate their efforts on Fiji and the LMS on Samoa.
However, the dedication of individual Wesleyans, like Peter
Turner, and the existence of close social and political ties
between Samoa and Tonga meant that the comity arrangement
was soon a dead letter.[15]

For forty years after the opening of their missions in
Fiji and Samoa, the Wesleyans (known increasingly in this
period as the Methodists) made no attempt to open new areas
in the South Pacific.[16] The Wesleyan Church in England was
weakened by internal controversy and declining

membership.[17]   It   was   decided,   therefore,   in   1854   to
transfer responsibility for missionary work in Australia and
the   Pacific   to   the   newly   independent   Methodist   General
Conference   of   Australasia.   The   Conference's   meager
resources were barely sufficient to sustain the existing
missions in Fiji, Samoa, Tonga and New Zealand, let alone
break new ground.

In   1874   Dr.   George   Brown,   a   Methodist   missionary   in
Samoa, managed to persuade the executive committee of the
Conference to allow him to recruit islander missionaries for
work in western Melanesia.   The following year he selected
nine   missionaries   from   Fiji,   Samoa,   and   Rotuma   and
established   a   station   at   Duke   of   York   Island   near   New
Britain.

Samoan missionaries had already seen service in the
Ellice Islands, where the first LMS party came ashore in
1865.   To the north, in the Gilberts, the ABCFM had been at
work since 1857.[18]   Founded in Massachusetts in 1810, the
"Boston Mission" was a Calvinist expression of the Great
Revival.   Adherents were committed to "sharing the message
of salvation with all nations," and by 1819 the ABCFM was on
its way to Hawaii.[19]   Like the LMS the ABCFM made use of
islander   converts   and   sent   Hawaiian   teachers   to   the
Gilberts.   Those teachers were not particularly effective,
and by 1890 the ABCFM was shouldered aside by the more
aggressive and accommodating Sacred Heart Mission.

Roman Catholic orders were not always so successful.
The   Marists,   for   example,   suffered   terrible   setbacks   in
Melanesia.   They   were   robbed,   murdered,   and   undone   by
disease while working in New Caledonia, the Solomons, and
New Guinea during the 1840s.   Their prospects were bleak,
and it was often only their "rigidly exclusive" view of
Christianity and their willingness--indeed readiness--to die
for their cause that sustained them.[20]

During the second quarter of the nineteenth century the
Roman Catholics divided Oceania into a number of Vicariates
Apostolic. The Church of England sought to demarcate its
own operational area in the southwest Pacific in 1841, but
an error in the Letters Patent had the effect of extending
the boundary of the diocese of the Bishop of New Zealand
northward to include most of Melanesia. The church's
mission to the islands, the Melanesian Mission, operated
indirectly through islander converts and it was not until
1896 that the Mission established a school in the
Solomons.[21]

"RATHER EARTHY MEDIATORS"

The Protestant and Roman Catholic missions began their
labours in the period between the age of exploration and the
age of annexation. It was a time during which islanders
came into increased contact with the outside world through
the visits of whaling ships, sandalwood cutters, beche-de-
mer fishers, and traders. In addition, many islanders saw
service on board European vessels and not a few European and
American sailors decided, willingly or unwillingly, to come
ashore.

The Polynesian islands, in particular, had their fair
share of beachcombers and castaways. These men, as Dening
and Maude have shown, were marginal figures occupying the
intersecting margins of two worlds.[22] Janus-like, they
looked both ways, interpreting the island world for the
Europeans and vice-versa. Acquaintance with the mores,
methods, and material culture of the European world enabled
these "rather earthy mediators" to provide a "preliminary
softening" of the "fatal impact."[23]

Willy-nilly beachcombers came to live like their hosts.
But no matter how acculturated the visitors became, they
challenged and changed the existing order. While it could

be argued that certain taboos or prohibitions were inapplicable to beachcombers because their gods were different, the visitors' "contempt for local gods and apparent immunity from the consequences . . . created a general skepticism--a readiness for change--" which paved the way for missionary endeavors.[24]

In a number of cases, beachcombers took a direct hand in promoting Christianity. When John Williams paid his second visit to Samoa in October 1832, he discovered that two English sailors on Upolu had already been hard at work proselytizing. The men claimed to have converted roughly three hundred Samoans. One of them described his activities to Williams:

> "Why, Sir, I goes about and talks to the people, and tells 'em that our God is good, and theirs in bad; and when they listens to me, I makes 'em religion, and baptizes 'em.... I takes water, and dips my hand in it, and crosses them in their foreheads and in their breasts, and then I reads a bit of a prayer to 'em in English." "Of course," I said, "they understand you." "No," he rejoined, "but they says they knows it does 'em good."[25]

Elsewhere, in the Ellice Islands, traders set themselves up as missionaries on Niutao and Niu in the 1860s. They enforced observance of the Sabbath, made laws, and collected fines and church dues in coconut oil.[26] Their efforts generated "a great interest in Christianity and . . . an unusual willingness to accept the precepts and practices laid down by the [LMS] missionaries.[27]

For the most part, the involvement of Europeans was less direct. There are many examples of such men acting as intermediaries in mission encounters. When an ABCFM group stopped at Butaritari in the Gilberts on their way to the Marshalls in 1852, Richard Randell, a coconut oil trader, acted as interpreter. Still later, when the ABCFM decided to establish a permanent presence in the Gilberts, they selected Abaiang for their headquarters, not only because it was near other populous islands, but because Captain Ichabod Handy, the master of the Fairhaven whaler, Belle, was friendly with the most powerful chief.[28]

In the case of Tahiti it was the withdrawal of European support that contributed indirectly to the success of the LMS mission. In 1802, Peter Haggerstein, a Swedish beachcomber, secured the support of castaways from the brig Norfolk to keep the Tahitian chief, Pomare I, in power. When the crew of the Norfolk and castaways from the Margaret left Tahiti, Pomare's son, Pomare II, with few Europeans available to fight for him, obliged to withdraw to Moorea in 1808. There, in desperation, he turned to Christianity.[29]

Not infrequently, cooperation between missionaries and other Europeans gave way to avoidance or hostility. Many of the latter, like Haggerstein, had secured positions of privilege and prestige within island society.[30] Indeed, their existence depended upon their value as mercenaries, interpreters, artisans, advisers, and procurers of trade goods. Missionaries threatened to eclipse these Europeans by opposing their military activities and by replacing them in middleman and commercial realms. Whalers and traders in Tonga, for instance, accused the Wesleyans of encouraging the Tongans to drive tougher bargains in the pork and produce trade.[31]

Much of this antipathy was rooted in fundamentally different lifestyles and visions of the world. Europeans tended to view missionaries as intolerant, naive, sanctimonious busybodies. Missionaries, for their part, were dismayed by the gambling, whoring and drinking proclivities of resident Europeans. Reverend J. E. Newell complained about the "'abominable and wicked practices' of gin-selling foreigners" on Nikunau in the southern Gilberts,[32] while John Williams decried "the common sailors

. . . the very vilest of the whole" who debauched the islanders.[33] Some Europeans responded by opposing mission activities, which discouraged sales of liquor, and attempted to regulate the lives of the beach community in accordance with stifling moral codes.[34] What the actors failed to realize, more often than not, was the fact that, wittingly or unwittingly, they were working toward the same goal--the transformation of island society to meet their respective needs. Beachcombers created a spiritual vacuum that missionaries sought to fill, while missionaries, by promoting a Christian, capitalist, and democratic ethos, created a set of conditions favoring commercial and colonial activity. The evidence suggests, then, that the undermining of the traditional fabric of island society was a necessary prerequisite to rapid conversion.[35] This appears to have been the case in the Gilbert and Ellice Islands: In the southern Gilberts and in the Ellice, where the frequency of contact with Europeans was much higher than in the central and northern Gilberts, Christianity was quickly adopted. Not so in the central and northern Gilberts. There, Christianity, as advanced by the ABCFM in the 1870s and 1880s, was not considered relevant in terms of the islanders' fundamental concern, the working out of traditional political rivalries. Christianity simply did not fulfill a need at the time. It did not constitute a sufficiently attractive strategy to justify overthrowing the old order, which, in Burkean terms, enjoyed the advantage of being tested and true. It was not until the labor trade, naval law, and colonial rule transformed Gilbertese society that the alien ideology made "sense in their own terms."[36]

"A VALUABLE POINT OF ENTRY"

While beachcomers and other Europeans contributed to the success or failure of missionary endeavours, so did what we might call "returnees." Returnees were Pacific Islanders

who came home, following a period of residence or service
abroad, or who fetched up in other parts of the Pacific by
accident or design. Some had been converted during their
absence, some only had a passing acquaintance with the Word.
There were not many returnees, but they played an important
part in spreading the gospel and contributing to the
preliminary softening.

Catholic involvement in Tonga was determined in part by
returnees. A group of Tongans had converted to Catholicism
during a two-year stay on Wallis. When they decided to
return to Tongatapu in the early 1840s, they requested the
services of a priest. Bishop Pompallier was happy to
oblige, as he realized that the migrants constituted "a
valuable point of entry" into Tongan society.[37]

Twenty years later, Elekana, an LMS teacher from
Manihiki in the northern Cooks, drifted by canoe to
Nukulaelae in the Ellice Islands.[38] He stayed there some
time and then, returning to Samoa, convinced the LMS to send
a mission party to the Ellice Islands. The Reverend A.W.
Murray responded to this request and took mission teachers,
including Elekana, to Nukulaelae, Funafuti, and Nui in
1865.[39]

Returned laborers introduced Catholicism to Nanumea and
Funafuti in the 1870s. Adherence to Catholicism was as much
an expression of opposition to the power of Samoan pastors
there as it was an illustration of religious commitment.
Farther north, variations on Roman Catholicism were
introduced to the Gilberts by laborers returning from Tahiti
and Samoa. One of them styled himself a prophet and
developed an enthusiastic Catholic following at Tewai
village on Tabiteuea, where Tioba (Jehovah) was symbolized
by feather-covered crosses.[40] These exercises, while often
little less than "garbled parodies" of Christianity, paved

the way for the successful Sacred Heart assault on the ABCFM position in the Gilberts.[41]

Elsewhere, Catholic labors were facilitated by one-time sailors. When Bishop Pompallier visited Futuan in 1837, one of the men who came aboard was Keletaona, whose father had been one of the two chiefs who ruled the island. Keletaona had served for five years on an Australian whaler and requested the bishop to leave missionaries behind to instruct the people of Futuna.[42] The same thing happened in the Solomons. Following the death of Bishop Epalle on Santa Isabel in 1845, the remainder of the Marist party removed to San Cristobal. There they met a local man, Loukou, who had been a cabin boy on an English ship. Loukou urged the missionaries to settle in his village and, although they chose not to, he continued to be of value as a go-between.[43]

"A CLIMATE OF READINESS"

The receptivity of Oceanic peoples to aliens and their ideas and the degree of coincidence that existed between traditional and imported value systems set the stage for missionary enterprises.[44] Maude comments upon the "exceptional receptivity" of Polynesians and Micronesians to outsiders, and while contact accounts contain episodes of treachery and murder there is much to support his view.[45] There is certainly less evidence of receptivity in Melanesia, perhaps because there were few European residents there before the missionaries arrived. Melanesia is a malarial zone and its inhabitants enjoyed a fearsome reputation.[46] What the Melanesians did experience, however, were the extensive effects of the labor trade.[47] That trade (1863-1911) exposed upwards of 100,000 Melanesians to the European world, and increased Melanesian receptivity to Christianity.[48] There was relatively little recruitment in New Guinea, however, and the Solomons, which bore the brunt

of the trade, were not subject to missionary labors--save
those of the Melanesian Mission--until the very end of the
period under review.

Not only was the receptivity of Melanesian societies
lower but there was a smaller coincidence between
traditional belief systems and Christianity than in
Polynesia. Melanesian subsistence agriculturalists and
fisherfolk lived in a world without religious or political
hierarchies. Their lives were affected by sorcery, magic,
and the machinations of ancestral spirits and ghosts. They
were less given to concerning themselves with genealogies
than the Polynesians and the concepts of mana and tapu (or
their rough equivalents) played a smaller part in their
daily round, particularly in the islands to the west of
Fiji.

LMS missionary laborers in the Cooks resulted in the
alternation, rather than the replacement of many major pre-
contact religious concepts. "To the Rarotongans," Gilson
writes, "the white missionaries were virtually superhuman,"
and it was not difficult for the Cook Islanders to accept
the fact that the missionary god, Jehovah, was sufficiently
omnipotent to displace traditional dieties.[49] Moreover,
Jehovah became the new and most important source of mana
ariki, or chiefly power, since the mana of the old dieties
seemed "no longer worth taking seriously."[50] Such chiefly
power--without direct equivalency in Melanesia--was easily
comprehended by European missionaries raised in cultures
where monarchs were god's lieutenants on earth and defenders
of the faith.

In addition, the islanders found Old Testament
genealogies and strict spiritual injunctions compatible with
their own concerns about kinship and tapu. They became
specialists in the Old Testament, reconciling or ignoring
those portions of the Biblical story that did not coincide

with their own past. Indeed, critics of the conversion
process have argued that "many islanders merely added
Jehovah to their pantheon of dieties and the missionaries to
the [Cook Islands] hierarchy of chiefs."[51]
     The same could also be said of Samoa where
"Christianity, instead of bursting the bonds of the old life
[had] been eaten up by it."[52] The success of the LMS
enterprise arose in large part from a dialectical process of
accommodation in which Samoan society became Christianized
and the LMS brand of Christianity became politicized. This
process was made possible by the fortuitous coincidence
between the organizational structure of the LMS and the pre-
contact socio-political environment.
     From the outset, the LMS missionaries concentrated
their efforts on converting the Samoan chiefs in the hope
that such conversions would give rise to "people movements,"
the wholesale embracing of the new religion.[53] In so doing
the missionaries were drawn into "an arena in which
political relations, consisting of labile alignments of
chiefs, descent groups, villages and districts, shaped the
mission's administrative organization, procedures, affairs
and autonomy."[54] In short, as Tiffany points out, "the
missionaries' concern with their flock's spiritual welfare
inevitably meant intervention in internal political affairs,
which in turn influenced the structure and organization of
the mission enterprise."[55]
     The absence in Samoa of a priestly hierarchy of the
sort that prevailed in pre-contact Tahiti and the
localization of village and household dieties under chiefly
protection coincided neatly with the LMS's decentralized
organization and local congregational approach to
unconverted peoples.[56] Furthermore, the administrative
levels of the LMS in Samoa "largely coincided with the
traditional district and subdistrict levels of political
organization."[57] While the political aspects of the

conversion process are more properly reserved to the section
of this paper dealing with island politics, Douglas Oliver's
words are worth noting in passing:

> In Samoa, where religion was never so highly
> institutionalized as elsewhere in Polynesia, the
> mission teachers simply replaced native priests in
> the new system, and the matais [chiefs], formerly
> the families' intercessors with supernatural
> forces, simply became deacons in village churches.
> Ultimately the Protestant congregations developed
> into peculiarly Samoan native-church
> possessing many local twists in doctrine and
> practice.[58]

While the social and political environment might be
favorable to conversion, there were dimensions of the
message which the islanders frequently found indigestible.
Missionaries tended to emphasize miraculous events in an
effort to demonstrate God's power. Acceptance of such
miracles was, initially at least, beyond most listeners.
They were quite prepared, as MacDonald demonstrates with
reference to the Gilbertese, to embrace the idea of divine
intervention in the affairs of men, but to accept the idea
of the virgin birth or walking on water was to ask the
impossible.[59]   Such   concepts—and   abstractions   like
transubstantiation—were   greeted   with   looks   of   blank
incomprehension or hoots of derision. Their acceptance as
acts of faith usually followed conversion. What is
important to note here is that while ideas like divine
intervention, tapu, and mana found reassuring parallels in
Christian ideology, the existence of miracles and complex
abstractions probably hindered the conversion process.[60]

"ACCESSORY TO HIS VANITY"

The receptivity of Oceanic societies to the missionary
message was dictated to a substantial degree by indigenous
politics. As we have seen in the case of Samoa, the
missionaries sought to gain access to the principal power

brokers, chiefs in Polynesia, big-men in Melanesia. Mission success was dependent upon the individual chief's vision of the potency of traditional gods and his assessment of the value of the imported ideology in terms of advancing his political ambitions. There were difficult decisions and grave risks involved for both parties. The missionaries, ignorant for the most part of the customs, language, and political realities of the hosts, had to decide which chief to back. If one's chiefly patron fell on hard times the mission could be doomed. The chief, for his part, had to weigh carefully what the political market would bear. Would the new ideology, with its promise of access to European goods, expertise, and power serve as an "accessory to his vanity,"[61] promoting his cause and constituting a rallying cry for his followers? Or would the rejection of the traditional dieties cause his supporters to fade away and disaster to fall?

Initial chiefly response to the missionary presence was usually one of polite resistance. There were personal, practical, and ideological reasons for this reaction. Firstly, missionaries, convinced of the superiority of their culture and the infallibility of their cause, could be unpleasant.[62] They were not above being racist, overbearing, and condescending. Secondly, their presence threatened the status quo. While some chiefs and traditional priests might benefit thereby, others stood to lose. And thirdly, missionary teaching was inherently antithetical to the premises on which chiefly power was based. Missionaries--particularly those of non-conformist persuasions--argued that all men were equal in the sight of God. Furthermore, they expected chiefs and commoners alike to obey them in all spiritual matters. In practice, chiefs were remarkably adept at retaining their power, while in theory, the democratic dimensions of Christianity favored

the common folk. It is hardly surprising, therefore, that
chiefs entertained some reservations about the missionary
enterprise.

The careers of Pomare II, who supported LMS efforts in
Tahiti, and Taufa'ahau (later King George Tupou I) who sided
with the Wesleyans in Tonga, illustrate the close
relationship between indigenous politics and the success or
failure of missionary enterprises. LMS personnel arrived in
Tahiti expecting to seek the protection of "King" Pomare I.
What they failed to appreciate--misled as they were by the
accounts of early explorers--was that Tu, or Pomare I, did
not enjoy unchallenged supremacy over the islands. Instead
they discovered that he was fighting for his life.[63] Not
only were rival chiefs attempting to undermine his authority
in the western part of the archipelago, but Tahitian custom
obliged him to share his power increasingly with his son,
the Younger Tu (Pomare II after 1803). Far from being a
peaceful kingdom, Tahiti was a cockpit of intrigue and
warring factions. Garrett describes the dilemmas faced by
the missionaries working in this subtly structured and
unpredictable society:

> The missionaries found in time that as protégés of
> Pomare II they first had to work for his
> conversion, then share the sharp reversal of his
> fortunes in war, as exiles with him on the island
> of Moorea and in the Leeward Group. They had to
> resist Pomare's urgent attempt to get them to
> obtain firearms for his wars; at the same time
> they could not help being desperately anxious for
> his ultimate success. They were appalled by his
> chiefly sexual conduct with both men and women, by
> his addiction to alcohol and by his early
> indifference to their moral objections to
> infanticide and human sacrifice. But they knew
> they had to stay with him; if they could convert
> him they would probably witness a landslide in
> favour of their preaching on Tahiti, Moorea and
> Raiatea....[64]

The struggle for political paramountcy was inextricably bound up with the religious system: "The present national religion," the missionary Davies wrote, "is so blended with the civil concerns, or the privileges and authority of the chiefs, that they have no conception the one can stand without the other.[65]

Crucial to Pomare's fortunes were his links with 'Oro, the god of fertility and war centered on the great marae (ceremonial stone platform and temple compound) of Opoa on Raiatea. "'Oro was ceremonially necessary to validate assumption of tribal titles, and, secondly, continued provision of tribute and human sacrifices as acknowledgement that Pomare II was ari'i rahi [high chief] in substance as well as name."[66]

In 1808 Pomare's opponents forced him and his missionary supporters to flee to Moorea. Chastened by this reverse, Pomare questioned 'Oro's power. He was not alone in doubting the god's efficacy. Some of the marae had begun to fall into disrepair and longstanding rituals had been dispensed with or modified. Pomare's offer to abandon 'Oro and embrace Christianity (an offer reinforced by the destruction of his rivals in battle in 1815) must be seen against a backdrop of:

> a certain war-weariness with the futility of ritual sacrifices, raid and counter raid, and a search for the answer to the predicament of Tahitian politics - namely how to exercise power in a hierarchical and tribal society without continually alienating status rivals at one level and suppliers of produce and manpower at another.[67]

As in Tahiti, so in Tonga. When the LMS recommenced their efforts in the 1820s they found Tongan society riven by chiefly rivalry. Those chiefs who had been successful had no reason to doubt the validity of the old order. "My mind is fixed," announced one great Tongan leader, Ata, to visiting missionaries. "It is very good for you to attend

to your God and I will attend to mine, but I will not attend
to yours."[68] Less fortunate rivals, however, came to see
the traditional cosomology as "no longer adequate to explain
the new technical age ushered in by European contact."[69]
The apparent impotence of their gods predisposed them to
embrace Christianity.

The breakthrough occurred when Taufa'ahau, the ruler of
the Ha'apai Group in central Tonga, decided to convert in
1831. This decision was "the greatest asset the mission-
aries   gained   in   their   struggle   to   establish
Christianity."[70] Taufa'ahau's rivals allied themselves to
the Catholic cause--a cause that added a further element of
legitimacy to their political opposition. However, in the
end, George Tupou prevailed. Aided by and aiding the LMS,
he established hegemony over Tonga in 1852.

PRIESTLY OPPOSITION

Chiefs   were   not   the   only   elites   concerned   with
maintaining the status quo. The other major power brokers
were   the   traditional   priests,   who   realized   from   the
beginning that:

> The acceptance of Christianity, with its stronger
> and more sophisticated order of priesthood, meant
> the decline and in due course the disappearance of
> the traditional priesthood, together with all the
> power, honour, and privileges it members had
> enjoyed for centuries. This was an intolerable
> loss and , as might be expected, the members of
> the old order were prepared to put up a fight to
> retain the position.[71]

But it was not merely anxiety about preserving their
own privileges and power and that led Tongan priests to
oppose the papalangi's message so vigorously. They were
genuinely concerned about the way in which that message
threatened to destroy the group cohesion on which the
vitality   and   survival   of   Tongan   society   depended.

Furthermore, as repositories and interpreters of sacred
knowledge, they were committed to the maintenance of custom
and taboo, the abandonment or violation of which would
surely mean disaster.

The priests in the Cook Islands assured the LMS
Tahitian teacher that the idols he sought to destroy were
"the material link between the people and their deities and
that their destruction would be followed by dire catastro-
phes, most probably the extinction of the island's
population."[72] Similarly, in the southern Gilberts and
Ellice Islands, LMS personnel encountered resistance from
traditional priests who were concerned about the loss not
only of spiritual and temporal power but of wealth derived
from contributions. Priests were usually the last to
convert in the Ellice Islands. Macdonald illustrates this
point by reference to the last two pagans on Niutao in
1880s. They were both former priests who allowed their
families to attend church but preferred to live out their
days worshipping the old gods. [73]

"NO SONG, NO DANCE"

The success or failure of missionary enterprises in
Oceania was determined to a considerable degree by the
social, religious, and ideological backgrounds from which
the missions sprang. Such things as attitudes toward the
education of mission personnel, conversion strategies, lack
of staff, and funding had a profound effect on the outcome
of Christian labors.

Starting from the assumption that all things were
possible to God, the Wesleyans and LMS tended to view
serious training for missionary work irrelevant and
unnecessary. The formative years of the LMS were dominated
by the mission's "prime ideologist," Dr. Thomas Haweis.[74]

While his personnel policy would be challenged later by the
Reverend David Bogue, it prevailed during the conversion
phase of LMS labors in Tahiti. Haweis was convinced that:

> the best kind of men to reach simple though
> benighted savages, lost in superstition, would be
> members of the British lower classes who worked
> with their hands and could rapidly prepare the
> ground for the religious conversion of their
> pupils by teaching them useful arts and trades.[75]

Of the thirty members of the LMS party dispatched to
Tahiti in 1797 only four were ordained missionaries. The
rest were "godly mechanicks," a curious assortment of
tradesmen and craftsmen, including a wheelwright, a hatter,
and a gentlemen's servant.[76] Haweis believed that these
"godly unlearned artisans" would soon be able to convert and
marry Tahitian women.[77] Little did he realize that the
latter might prove to be more successful missionaries,
seducing two of the unmarried men away from the faith. If
the missionaries' resolve was not to be tested in this way
it was to be tested in others, and eleven of the eighteen
who came to Tahiti chose to leave.[78]

In other cases it was the conversion strategy itself
which was at fault. The ABCFM shared with the Wesleyans a
suspicion of all amusements and recreations. As Macdonald
notes, ABCFM policy had little attraction for the
Gilbertese. Robert Louis Stevenson described it as "no
song, no dance, no liquor, no alleviate of life--only toil
and church-going."[79] In particular, "the prohibition of
tobacco gave the mission little chance of success among a
people addicted to its use."[80] The Catholics, by
comparison, were more tolerant about Gilbertese culture and
even went so far as to pay for food and labor with tobacco.

George Augustus Selwyn, the first Bishop of New
Zealand, saw the Melanesian Mission as a vehicle enabling

"the Church of England [to] freely demonstrate the validity
of its spiritual claims and rebuild itself on a more perfect
model, closer to the church of antiquity."[82] Unfortunately,
his mission policy was sufficiently controversial that it
cut him off from the main sources of missionary and
financial support in the church. Undeterred, he pursued
what amounted to a "religious mirage," recruiting
Melanesians for conversion and training in New Zealand in
the 1850s.[83] From present day knowledge of Melanesia,
Hilliard concludes:

> [with] its complex languages, divergent
> subcultures and egalitarian social groupings
> Selwyn's confident expectation that he could
> engineer the conversion of up to 200,000 people by
> means of a central school, a cruising schooner and
> an army of youthful English-trained evangelists--
> and at a time before the invading European
> political and economic order had begun to interact
> on a decisive scale with the indigenous cultures--
> must be seen as a quixotic exercise, foredoomed to
> failure.[84]

Lack of staff was another problem that hindered missionary work. The LMS found its Cook Islands labors in
jeopardy when the three paramount ariki or chiefs of
Rarotonga each demanded a white missionary.[85] Similarly,
the Wesleyans in Tonga were hard pressed to know how to
consolidate their gains following the mass acceptance of
Christianity in Ha'apai and Va'vau in the early 1830s.

Funding was a perennial mission concern as well.
Financial constraints obliged the LMS to reduce the number
of missionaries in Samoa and to depend more heavily on
Samoan teachers. The LMS went still farther in Tahiti. The
first sixteen years of the mission's operation there
absorbed 47 percent of the LMS's global expenditure.[86] The
only way the mission fathers could recruit more staff was to

enter into "a curious mixture of religion and trade" with
the Reverend Samuel Marsden in New South Wales.[87] Marsden,
a Church of England cleric, was known to be "industrious,
financially astute and fully in sympathy with the [LMS]
Mission Society."[88] He organized a pork and produce trade
with the missionaries, an arrangement that the LMS directors
noted "would soon cover the whole expence [sic] of
equipment, and provide for the support of the mission."[89]

A "FRUCTIFYING SUPPLEMENT"

The Pacific is a maritime world where great distances
separate island groups. Yet even greater distances
separated the various missions from their metropolitan
bases. Travel was, perforce, by ship, and missions secured
their own vessels--like the Melanesian Mission's Southern
Cross or the LMS's Messenger of Peace--or chartered them as
the Marists did when they travelled aboard the Marian Watson
to Santa Isabel or the Mary Ann to Rooke Island. But these
vessels could not afford the missionaries protection, and
since there were few imperial administrations in the South
Pacific during this period, missionary organizations had to
rely upon visiting warships. Gunboats--principally of the
British and French navies--provided transport, protection,
and prestige, but the relationship between the men of the
blue and the men of the cloth was tinged with ambivalence.

Gunboats were of great value to missionaries as symbols
of power. Many Tongans, for example,"reasoned that if the
God of the white people could make . . . men of war and
their guns and powder, it must be true that He was the only
God."[90] What is more, the respect paid to missionaries by
naval officers and the apparent ability of missionaries to
command the presence of warships suggested a level of mana
appropriate to the representatives of a great god.

The presence of naval vessels or the threat of their arrival had a profound impact on missionary labors. During the civil war in Tonga in the 1840s, the Wesleyans appealed to Captain Croker of HMS Favourite for assistance. This he was willing to give, but he and several of his officers were killed storming the heathen redoubt at Pea. Nevertheless, the Ha'a Havea chiefs, fearful that Croker's death would occasion reprisals by another British man-of-war, agreed to cease fighting and peace was restored. Similarly, during the last stages of that conflict in 1852 the Marists sought French naval support from Tahiti. The ship that arrived, however, was not French but British, HMS Calliope. The Catholics were so disheartened by this turn of events that resistance to George Tupou collapsed.[91]

Despite such reverses, French naval support proved to be "a vital and fructifying supplement" to Marist labours.[92] The Catholics in Tonga always welcomed the visits of French gunboats because they helped counter Wesleyan allegations that the Marists were "outcasts from their own people."[93] Want of such support was thought to have contributed to Father Chanel's death on Futuna in 1841. Concerned that a similar fate might befall him and that the schooner on which he was travelling to recover Chanel's remains might be attacked, Bishop Pompallier judged it "wise and prudent" to request a French navy escort.[94] Bishop Collomb was of like mind. "Above all else," he wrote to his superior, "it is the dangers to which we shall be exposed [in the Solomons] that have prompted me--in spite of earlier repugnance to do so--to request a visit by a ship of state."[95]

The Melanesian Mission also relied heavily upon the navy. In Bishop George Augustus Selwyn's view, "the 'effectual conversion and civilization' of Melanesia could

only be achieved by a combination of 'the two forces of
religion and law,' with the latter in the form of a
permanent and enlightened British naval presence."[96] Selwyn
made his first visits to southern Melanesia accompanied by
British gunboats, HMS Havannah in 1849 and HMS Fly in 1850.
Later, in the 1860s, the Southern Cross was accompanied by
HMS Curacoa and from the 1870s "a regular pattern of
cooperation evolved, based on practical necessity and common
loyalties."[97]

     This relationship, however, was an ambivalent one.
"Missionaries don't go as British subjects," Bishop Patteson
of the Melanesian Mission declared, "but as Ministers of
[Christ] to the heathen, and must not mix up the two characters."[98] But mix them up they did, and missionaries of
whatever persuasion enjoyed and usually expected the
protection provided by men-of-war. What they reserved for
themselves was the luxury of taking the moral high ground,
of decrying the process by which protection was provided.
They sought by a variety of means--some more fictional than
sincere--to distance themselves from the punitive aspects of
naval work. Thus when Marist missionaries, rescued from
Poebo Station on New Caledonia in 1847, heard that the
captain of the French warship Brillante was planning a
punitive expedition ashore, they completely disassociated
themselves "from every aspect of this act of vengeance
against the people who did us evil. . . ."[99] The Anglican
missionaries were somewhat less emphatic and it was
generally agreed that they should help Royal Navy officers
maintain peace in the islands provided that they, the
missionaries, did not associate personally with bombardments
or other punitive measures.[100]

"AN EXTREMELY SIGNIFICANT ROLE"

     What missionary accounts frequently overlook is the
"extremely significant role" of island mission teachers or

pastors in spreading the Word.[101] Almost certainly the initial impetus for employing converts in this way was practical rather than ideological in origin. Missions like the LMS did not have the staff to spread the gospel without assistance. Other arguments obtained later. South Sea islanders, it was said, would be more understanding of and acceptable to their indigenous hosts. Furthermore, island teachers would be less expensive to maintain in the field since their tastes were simple and easily fulfilled. And they would be able to communicate sympathetically the realities of their own conversions.

The employment of island teachers was an LMS, ABCFM, and Wesleyan strategy. The Melanesian Mission, as we have seen, had its own variation on island teachers, while the Roman Catholics resisted their employment on the grounds that only those well versed in Latin, Greek, and canonical matters could serve as priests.[102]

The first LMS missionaries to reside in the Cooks were two Society Islanders, one of whom, Papeiha, accomplished "more in Rarotonga in two years than English missionaries in Tahiti had in twenty."[103] Papeiha married the daughter of Tinomana and took a title under that chief. Tinomana and his Aorangi people had been beset by enemies, and when Papeiha destroyed the idols of a major chief with impunity Tinomana was persuaded to switch his allegiance to the new and seemingly more powerful god.[104]

The ABCFM employed a strategy in the Gilberts similar to the one developed by the Melanesian Mission following the failure of the latter's first conversion campaign--a strategy of reassurance and support whereby missionaries paid regular visits to island teachers in the field. The Anglicans compared their approach to the use of white corks on a black net. The ABCFM's black net was a fraternity of Hawaiian teachers dispatched to the northern and central

Gilberts. The Hawaiian missionaries were, for the most part, men "of little education and limited theological training."[105] They made relatively little headway against the entrenched traditions of the Gilbertese. Elsewhere, however, in the southern Gilberts and in the Ellice, where different conditions prevailed, the LMS made rapid progress. The Polynesian pastors engaged by the mission led "a vigorous assault against the forces of darkness and propounded a Samoanized form of Christianity that had a greater appeal for islanders than the doctrines and lifestyle advocated by most European missionaries."[106]

While island teachers were generally successful in converting other islanders, they were not above being corrupted by their new-found power. Williams for example, was disturbed to find his Polynesian colleagues in the Cooks holding positions "comparable to those of hereditary chiefs of high standing," though European missionaries were later held in even higher esteem.[107] Similarly, the Hawaiian missionary, Kapu, became the effective ruler of Eita village in northern Tabiteuea in the 1870s and carried all before him with the sword. The Samoan pastors in the Ellice Islands, the Solomons, and New Guinea occasionally tended to be overbearing and insensitive. Not only were they proud of their culture, the fa'a-Samoa, but they were convinced of its superiority. Moreover, they enjoyed considerable power and privilege at home and expected to be accorded the same in the field.[108]

"UNSEEMLY COLLISIONS"

Inter- and intra-mission rivalry had a profound effect on mission labors in the South Pacific. While the most obvious and destructive rivalry prevailed between the Catholics and Protestants, Protestant missions were not above challenging one another. Sharp clashes occurred within missions as a result of tensions between European missionaires and island pastors or over differences concerning mission strategy.

Rigidly exclusive views of Christianity lay at the heart of Catholic-Protestant rivalry. While Protestant missions like the LMS and Wesleyans differed fundamentally on certain theological issues, they were prepared to coexist, albeit uneasily at times.[109] The Catholics, however, would have none of this. They believed that the ignorance of the pagans, while lamentable, was as nothing compared to the heresy of the Protestants who were actively engaged in denying the islanders' eternal salvation. Under the circumstances, comity agreements were unthinkable, and "unseemly collisions" were inevitable.[110]

Complicating matters still further was the fact that the Catholics and Protestants viewed one another as the advanced guard for French and British imperialism, respectively. Thus, religious rivalry was exacerbated by national concerns. Conversely, at the island level, national concerns took on a religous complexion as rivals for political power sought to exploit the competition for souls to further their own ambition. Religious cooptation became a convenient strategy for advancement, and church organizations provided new arenas for acquiring status and working out traditional rivalries.

The Wesleyan missionaries in Tonga spent a "tremendous proportion" of their time fighting Roman Catholicism during the 1840s and 1850s.[111] Similiarly, there was "a bitter and destructive rivalry" between the Catholics and the ABCFM for half a century or more in the central and northern Gilberts.[112] In Samoa it was a matter of enforcing the comity agreement between the LMS and the Wesleyans. The

Wesleyans, reinforced from Tonga, were already a power in the land by the time the LMS arrived. Wesleyans could not be dislodged nor could they be ignored. They made "considerable inroads" on Savai'i, Manono, and Upolu in the 1830s,[113] and it was altogether appropriate that the first book published by the LMS in Samoa (A Talk About Different Religions, 1839) dealt with the competition for converts.

The relationship between European missionaries and island mission teachers could also be antithetical at times. The ABCFM, for example, was deeply dismayed by Kapu's crusade on Tabitieuea and repudiated his "deed of darkness," which involved decapitation of villagers who resisted the Hawaiian pastor's imposition of the Word.[114] The Board also expressed concern about the way in which the Hawaiian pastors or their relatives had become involved in commercial activities in the Gilberts.

Racialism contributed as well to the tensions between missionaries and pastors. Latukefu's research suggests that European missionaries condemned what they considered to be the "superior attitudes" of South Sea Islands' pastors to their flock. Further, it suggests that white missionaries considered island teachers and Melanesians alike "as black ... [and] as 'natives'."[115]

OTHER MISSIONS

The success or failure of missions in one part of the Pacific often affected the activities of missions in another. News of the success of LMS missionaries in Tahiti, for example, illustrated the value of perseverance and encouraged the Wesleyan Methodist Conference to dispatch Reverend Walter Lawry to Tonga in 1832.[116] Similarly, Papeiha, the Tahitian native teacher, was successful in the Cook Islands, partly because he was able to regale the

Rarotongan chiefs with stories of LMS exploits in Tahiti.
Bishop George Augustus Selwyn of the Melanesian Mission
travelled throughout the islands for two weeks in 1847
aboard HMS Dido. He was able to observe first hand Wesleyan
work in Tonga and LMS endeavors in Samoa. While as a High
Churchman he regarded "non-episcopal bodies as laying
outside the divinely constituted church," he was deeply
impressed by the expansive energy of Polynesian
Christianity" and by the employment of island teachers as
missionaries.[117]

Not all models were positive. The arrival of French
priests in Tahiti in 1837 and the subsequent annexation of
the island by France produced "a wave of apprehension" in
the Cooks. Cook Islanders greeted Catholics with hostility,
and the chiefs of Rarotonga requested British naval
protection in the event of a French move against the
Cooks.[118] The reaction was much the same in the Friendly
Islands. Tongans became increasingly concerned about the
long-term implications of Marist evangelism but drew heart
when they heard of the destruction of Marist mission
stations in New Caledonia in 1847. The news was said to
have been used to discredit Catholicism in Tonga as a "lotu
[faith] abandoned at the same time by God and by man."[119]

"THE MISSION WAS THE BISHOP"

Missions operated on a frontier where conditions
demanded strength of character. That strength was often a
determining factor in the outcome of missionary labors.
There was no lack of strong, forceful, egotistical
individuals in the mission world, and they left their stamp
on mission endeavors.

The renewal of Wesleyan or Methodist activity in the
South Pacific in the 1870s owed much to the resourcefulness

and determination of Dr. George Brown, who harried his
superiors "on every occasion" to send island teachers to
Melanesia.[120] For Reverend Nathaniel Turner it was not
drive but "a rare sensitivity and tact" that enabled him to
achieve so much in Tonga. His predecessor, Thomas, lacked
those traits and so alienated the chief, Ata, that the
latter forbade his people to worship or attend school.[121]

Reverend Samuel Marsden's strength lay elsewhere. It
was his financial acumen and commercial talents that enabled
him to rescue the ailing LMS mission in Tahiti. By way of
comparison, Hiram Bingham Jr., who served with the ABCFM in
the Gilberts, had no taste for trade and was, in fact, more
scholar than evangelist. What interested him was rescuing
individual souls rather than entire missions.

In the case of the Melanesian Mission, "the Mission was
the bishop."[122]   George Augustus Selwyn "dictated policy,
bound by no diocesan synod or council"[123]   A man of
"formidable exterior and imperious will,"[124]   Selwyn saw
himself "as a commanding general of an advancing Christian
army."[125] The success or failure of the mission was largely
of his making.

"YOU DO NOT WANT ME REALLY"

Most accounts of contact in the Pacific highlight the
importance of trade goods in the social and commercial
intercourse between Europeans and islanders. As members of
societies with modest inventories of tools and weapons and
social systems rooted in the acquisition and distribution of
wealth, the islanders were eager to acquire almost
everything the new comers had to offer. Moreover, the
islanders soon come to demand trade items in return for
goods and services. The missionaries were not exempt from
these demands, and trade goods appear to have played a key
role in the conversion process.

Trade goods also betokened a god of great power. A
Samoan chief employed this line of logic when he exhorted
his followers to embrace Christianity:

> Now I conclude that the God who has given to his
> white worshippers these valuable things must be
> wiser than our gods, for they have not given the
> like to us. We all want these articles; and my
> proposition is, that the God who gave them should
> be our God.[126]

The possession of trade goods and the nature of the
goods prossessed were issues of vital importance in terms of
establishing the mission beachhead. Father Verguet, a
Marist priest who served on San Cristobal in the 1840s,
describd the dilemma facing missionaries when they arrived
in an area for the first time. "If he arrives . . . without
bringing supplies, he will die from hunger and misery. But
if he should come with provisions, these arouse the cupidity
of the natives, who then will attack him, steal these goods
and kill him."[117]

Matters were not always so grim, but missionaries could
not afford to be without at least some items of trade. The
Roman Catholics in Tonga suffered from a lack of material
resources, while the Wesleyan missionaries soon discovered
that the favorable reception they received there was "due
more to [Reverend] Lawry's supply of goods then to his
teaching."[128]   Melanesian Mission personnel had much the
same experience on San Cristobal in the 1870s.   The
islanders were hospitable but the missionaries' welcome
"depended upon a constant supply of trade goods," and the
islander' reaction to Christian teaching was "one of
unchanging indifference."[129]   After a visit in 1872, R. S.
Jackson asked the Wango people if they wanted him to return:

> "Yes," cried they, "and bring very much tobacco,
> and axes, and beads and red braid." "Ah!" said I,
> "you do not want me really; you only want
> tobacco." At which they laughed.[130]

The unwillingness of the ABCFM to supply tobacco to the Gilbertese and of the LMS to provide Pomare with firearms worked against those missions. By way of contrast, the Sacred Heart missionaries were highly popular because they dispensed tobacco, books, medallions, and food fairly freely to the Gilbertese. Indeed, the latter explained their conversion to Captain Davis of HMS Royualist in "other than spiritual terms."[131] "Oh," observed one, "that Roman Catholic missionary man, he no trade [carry on commercial operations]--he no fine [as the ABCFM did for Sabbath and other infractions]--he give um book--no make pay. Oh, he belong good man."[132]

TOWERS OF BABEL

The Pacific Islands are home to roughly one-quarter of the world's languages. Almost all missionaries working in the area were confronted with the problem of mastering a local language or languages sufficiently well to communicate the Word, replete as it was with an assortment of theological concepts and abstractions. Until such mastery was achieved, all hope of effecting conversions was chimerical. Some missionaries did enjoy the advantage of previous exposure to an Oceanic language. Thus Reverend Nathaniel Turner's association with the Maoris of New Zealand enabled him to learn Tongan "quickly and thoroughly."[133] Similarly, Tahitian mission teachers working in the Cooks and Samoan pastors laboring in the Ellice Islands were able to benefit from the historical similarities of Polynesian languages. This was certainly not the case, however, when missionaries moved into Melanesia, where there were upwards of a thousand languages and dialects. Tongan and Samoan pastors were at the same disadvantage then as their European colleagues, and the Melanesian Mission was driven to adopt Mota from the Banks Islands as the lingua franca for all the different linguistic groups represented at the mission school on Norfolk Island.[134]

Hiram Bingham Jr.'s experiences as an ABCFM missionary in the Gilberts illustrates some of the problems associated with mastering an island language:

> No miraculous gift of tongue is now conferred upon the ambassadors of Christ. Like other mission-aries I have found no other way for the obtaining of my desire than to patiently set myself to work in picking up one word after another and one sentence after another of the heathen jargon which noisy savages were shouting about my ears.[135]

Pioneering missionaries like Bingham, Williams, and Turner not only learned local languages but performed the enormously valuable task of reducing them to written form. In each case this was a prelude to the production of the Bible or gospels. Turner saw the production of a Tongan Bible as "vital for the conversion of the people," while Williams and Bingham translated gospels into Rarotongan and Gilbertese.[136] Bingham's accomplishment was particularly remarkable since, despite absences, ill health, and poor eyesight, he was able to publish the New and the Old Testament in Gilbertese, the latter translated from the original Hebrew.[137]

EDUCATION

Closely related to the reduction of Oceanic languages to a written form were missionary efforts at education and publication. Most missionaries saw education as a vital vehicle for the promotion of conversion and the prevention of apostasy. "Education," however, was confined largely to those ends. What mission teachers sought to do was to inculcate a knowledge of the Bible and to develop a degree of literacy sufficient to combat superstition and give access to the scriptures.

Some missions were willing to teach English while others were not. In accordance with long established principles, the ABCFM was committed to educating Gilbertese

in their own language. This policy, while understandable,
discouraged conversion because the islanders, who had
developed an appreciation of the world beyond the reef,
wanted to learn English. The "King" of Abaiang, in fact,
was only prepared to send his son to the mission school if
the language of instruction was English.[138]

The dissemination of mission educational materials was
greatly facilitated by the arrival of printing presses in
the Pacific. The first printing press arrived in Tonga in
1831 and the first book printed there was published in the
same year.[139] Eight years later, the LMS established a
press in Samoa; by the end of 1845 almost eight million
pages of "useful reading material" had been published and
distributed throughout the group, thereby creating and
answering the demands of an increasingly literate
audience.[140] Printing and education helped spread the Word,
push back the frontiers of heathenish superstition, and keep
converts within the fold.

"MY TRIBUTE TO THE CLIMATE"

One of the biggest problems which the missionaries
faced, particularly in Melanesia, was that of health--their
own health and that of their flock. Few missionaries were
qualified medical practitioners. They did not advertise
themselves as such but were drawn, nevertheless, into treat-
ing the islanders for reasons of compassion, prestige, or
necessity. Islanders believed in a "direct connection
between the efficacy of medicine and the power and truth of
the gods."[141] Thus when missionaries failed to cure
maladies it was interpreted as a sign that Jehovah's mana
was no match for that of traditional deities or ancestral
spirits. Such was the case when Thomas, a Wesleyan
missionary, failed to cure Mataele, the son of the Tongan
chief Ata. Subsequently Mataele was taken to a traditional

god house and recovered. Temporarily, at least, faith in
the old gods was confirmed, and few dared flirt with the new
religion for fear that those gods, angered by impiety, might
visit ill-health upon the waverers.

Fortunately for the Wesleyan cause, other missionaries
were more successful than Thomas. "The success of the
Missionaries' medicine," Latukefu writes,

> dealt a fatal blow to heathenism, for while it was
> more difficult for the Tongans to comprehend many
> of the abstract principles of Christianity, they
> could easily see the beneficial effects of
> medicine especially when diseases were so
> prevalent and the death rate so high.[142]

When not attending to their flock, missionaries had
need to be concerned about their physical well-being. Early
Wesleyan efforts in Tonga were severely undermined by
Reverend Hutchinson's ill health, and Hiram Bingham Jr. was
so chronically unwell that he was repeatedly obliged to
leave the Gilberts. Malaria was the scourge in Melanesia.
It was perhaps "the most serious problem" the South Sea
Islands pastors had to face there.[143] None of them, coming
from malaria-free Polynesia, had any first-hand experience
with the disease or any concept of preventive medicine.
Lacking immunity, they sickened and died, often in a state
of blind resignation, convinced that their deaths were an
expression of God's will.

Catholic priests in the Solomons and New Guinea had
much the same outlook. "I, too, pay my tribute to the
climate," wrote Bishop Collomb as he and his colleagues
languished, fever ridden.[144] Collomb succumbed shortly
thereafter on Rooke Island in July 1848, the victim of fever
and a severe stomach disorder. His colleague, Father
Villien, was so shaken by Collomb's death that he too fell
ill and was overwhelmed by a combination of fever and
melancholy.

"VICTIMS OF THE FEROCITY"

No mission was quite as star-crossed as the Marist
Mission in Melanesia. Death was the missionaries' constant
companion, cutting short their efforts at conversion. In
July 1847 the New Caledonians laid siege to the Marist
station at Balade on the Baiaoup River. Six missionaries
made good their escape to a neighboring station at Poebo but
the seventh, Brother Marmoiton, was speared, clubbed, and
decapitated.[145]

Several weeks later, Bishop Collomb left New Caledonia
to visit San Cristobal, the only other island in the Western
Pacific where Catholic personnel were at work. When he
arrived he discovered, to his horror, that three of the four
men there had been hacked to death while the fourth had died
of fever.

Collomb, himself with less than a year to live,
stoically greeted these setbacks. These were not the first
Catholic martyrs in Melanesia. In December 1845 Bishop
Epalle, vicar Apostolic of Melanesia and Micronesia, had
gone ashore on Santa Isabel to establish a Marist station.
Prior to his departure, the Sydney press had warned
presciently that Epalle and his party would become "victims
of the ferocity of the peoples they intended to
evangelize,"[146] and, with all the certainty of a Greek
tragedy, Epalle was cut down with a tomahawk while he
parleyed with the islanders. "It seemed to me," Collomb
wrote, "that the losses which I suffered in New Caledonia
and the dangers which I encountered were nothing but simple
tests that God wanted to use to prepare me for the much
greater sacrifices to be encountered on my arrival in
Melanesia."[147]

DAME FORTUNE

Machiavelli revealed in The Prince how great men and
grand designs could be laid low by Dame Fortune. Even the
shrewdest and most opportunistic prince, he observed, could
be undone by a fickle and unpredictable twist of fate. So
it was with missionary labors.

LMS efforts in the Cooks, for example, suffered a sharp
setback in the early 1820s. Papeiha, the Tahitian mission
teacher, was on the verge of converting Vakaporo, a leading
chief, when Papeiha's assistant, Tiberio, was caught
fornicating with Vakaporo's betrothed daughter. Vakaporo
renounced Christianity immediately, but some years later the
mission's fortunes improved. A series of disastrous storms
and epidemics in 1830-31 killed off many of the opponents of
the new religion and convinced the remainder that this was
the way the Christian god punished non-believers.[148]

An even more remarkable stroke of good fortune befell
the LMS mission to Samoa. Only a few days before John
Williams put his eight Tahitian and Cook Islands teachers
ashore, Lei'ataua Tonumaipe'a Tamafaiga--whom Williams
considered the "devil chief" and main obstacle to the
introduction of Christianity--was assassinated.[149] While
there seems little doubt that the mission would have
ultimately prevailed despite Tamafaiga's presence, his
timely departure from the scene greatly facilitated the
mission's labors.

CONCLUSION

The object of this paper was the illustration of
variables affecting the outcome of the conversion phase of
missionary enterprises in the South Pacific during the
nineteenth century. The conversion process was analogous to
a set of scales. When the missionaries arrived in the
islands the scales were weighed heavily against them, borne
down by the weight of an entrenched and vital belief system.
That system, in turn, supported and was supported by society

in general and by traditional power brokers--chief, priests, and big men--in particular.

Missionaries were obliged to struggle against xenophobia, language problems, and difficult physical conditions in their efforts to establish a foothold and to interpret the bewildering complexities of indigenous social systems. Missionaries might or might not be assisted by resident Europeans, island converts, or naval personnel at this stage. Extensive contact with the outside world and a reasonable degree of coincidence between the imported message and traditional beliefs favored missionary efforts to tip the balance.

The key element, however, was the power broker's appreciation of the utility of their missionary presence. Only when the traditional system was sufficiently undermined that a new system was required to legitimize transformed local power structures and to explain the expanded universe did Christianity, in its various forms, make sense and have value. It was the islanders' changed appreciation of the validity of the old order that determined the moment when the scales shifted in the missionaries' favor. This was the moment of conversion. The missionaries were only one set of players in a much larger drama. While they were more committed to change than other Europeans and while the latter did play a part, it was the islanders who determined the success or failure of missionary efforts at conversion.

NOTES

I am particularly indebted to and have drawn heavily
upon the works of John Garrett, Richard Gilson, David
Hilliard, Hugh Laracy, Sione Latukefu, Barrie Macdonald,
H. E. Maude, and Sharon Tiffany.

[1]S. M. Creagh (LMS) to A. Tidman, August 1857, as
quoted in David Hilliard, God's Gentlemen, [St. Lucia,
Queensland, University of Queensland Press, 1978], 46.

[2]John Williams, A Narrative of Missionary Enterprises
in the South Sea Islands..., [London: John Snow, 1838], 582.

[3]As quoted in Sione Latukefu, "The Wesleyan Mission,"
in Friendly Islands: A History of Tonga, edited by Noel
Rutherford, [Melbourne: Oxford University Press, 1977],
122.

[4]Ibid., 130.

[5]Describing the conversion phase in Tahiti, Garrett
notes that:

Chiefs and commoners accept the otward forms of missionary
government and worship. But the external appearance of the
church was not a reliable clue to its internal character.
One of its functions was to protect part of the culture and
language of the Society Islands against the inroads of white
trade and conquest. The new religion became, by degrees, a
repository for elements of Tahitian language and custom, as
the older religions had been within pre-Christian society.
John Garrett, To Live Among the Stars: Christian Origins in
Oceania, [Geneva: World Council of Churches, 1982], 22.

[6]David Hilliard, "The South Sea Evangelical Mission in
the Solomon Islands: the Foundation Years," The Journal of
Pacific History, 4 (1969), 41-64, Roger Keesing, "Christians
and Pagans in Kwaio, Malaita," The Journal of the
Polynesian Society, 76 (1967), 82-100. I have confined
myself in this discussion to the problem of nominal conversion and have avoided trying to determine the occasion when
sincere faith—the "change of heart" much sought after by
missionaries—replaced a mechanical observance of Christian
forms. As Gilson points out:

The declaration of Christian intentions by the people
of Rarotonga did not entail immediate acceptance or understanding of the doctrine of personal salvation and the con-
fession of "sin." The tendency was rather that of an

expedient change of religious allegiance on the part of
various chiefs and some of their dependent priests, who
pulled their followers along with them, much as they had
before the Christian issue arose.

[7]The establishment of the LMS was greeted by the
Reverend David Bogue as the "funeral of bigotry." Garrett,
To Live Among the Stars, 10.

[8]Ibid., 8

[9]Stephen Neill, Colonialism and Christian Missions,
[New York: McGraw-Hill Book Company, 1966], 226.

[10]Gottfried Osterwal, "Introduction," in Mission,
Church, and Sect in Oceania, edited by James Boutilier et
al., [Ann Arbor: The University of Michigan Press, 1978],
31, Garrett, however, maintains that the establishment of "a
number of widely separated stations in the South Seas" was
part of the original LMS plan. Garrett, To Live Among the
Stars, 14.

[11]As quoted in Gilson, The Cook Islands, 26.

[12]Alan Tippett, People Movements in Southern
Polynesia: A Study in Church Growth, [Chicago: Moody Press,
1971], 111.

[13]The definitive work on Roman Catholic activities in
the Pacific in this period is Ralph Wiltgen's The Founding
of the Roman Catholic Church in Oceania 1825 to 1850,
[Canberra: Australian National University Press], 1979.

[14]Hugh Laracy, "The Catholic Mission," in Friendly
Islands: A History of Tonga, 137.

[15]John Garrett, "The Conflict Between the London
Missionary Society and the Wesleyan Methodists in mid-19th
Century Samoa," The Journal of Pacific History, 9 (1974),
65-80.

[16]Sione Latukefu, "The Impact of South Sea Islands
Missionaries on Melanesia," in Mission, Church, and Sect
in Oceania, 92.

[17]Garrett, "The Conflict ... Samoa," The Journal of
Pacific History, 9 (1974), 74.

[18]Barrie Macdonald, Cinderellas of the Empire: Towards
a History of Kiribati and Tavalu, [Canberra: Australian
National University Press], 1982, 31.

[19]Garrett, To Live Among the Stars, 10.

[20]Laracy, "The Catholic Mission," in Friendly Islands,
136.

[21]James Boutilier, "Missions, Administration and
Education in the Solomon Islands, 1893-1942," in Mission,
Church, and Sect in Oceania, 142.

[22]H. E. Maude, Of Islands and Men: Studies in Pacific
History, [Melbourne: Oxford University Press], 1968, and
Greg Dening, Islands and Beaches: Discourse on a Silent
Land, Marquesas 1774-1880, [Honolulu: The University Press
of Hawaii], 1980. In absolute terms, however, their numbers
were not large. There were only six beachcombers on the
island of Tahiti in 1800. Maude suggests that Samoa was
"the exception" as it was "virtually unvisited" until the
1820s, only a few years before the LMS arrived. Maude, Of
Islands and Men, 156.

[23]Ibid., 163.

[24]Ibid., 163.

[25]Williams, A Narrative of Missionary Enterprises, 421.

[26]Macdonald, Cinderellas of the Empire, 41.

[27]Ibid., 41.

[28]Ibid., 32

[29]Maude, Of Islands and Men, 158.

[30]Colin Newbury, Tahiti Nui: Change and Survival in
French Polynesia,1767-1948, [Honolulu: The University Press
of Hawaii], 1980, 11.

[31]Latukefu, "The Wesleyan Mission," in Friendly Islands,
118.

[32]Macdonald, Cinderellas of the Empire, 49.

[33]As quoted in Maude, Of Islands and Men, 164. Reverend
R. H. Codrington of the Melanesian Mission lamented the difficulties the mission encountered in recruiting islanders
for Norfolk Island because of "the prejudice against
missionary teaching which intercourse with the lower class
of Europeans [labor traders] always gives."

[34]Frank Even, a Frenchman trading on Nikunau in the
Gilberts in the late 1880s had good reason to support the

Catholic cause. He, an Irish trader, and the local
Gilbertese Catholics found themselves "the constant victims
of Protestant [ABCFM] intolerance." Macdonald, Cinderellas
of the Empire, 50.

[35]The Cook Islands, which were relatively untouched
prior to mission contact, are an obvious exception to this
rule, but the success of the LMS enterprise there is no
doubt explained in part by the favorable coincidence between
pre- and post-contact value systems.

[36]Macdonald, Cinderellas of the Empire, 40.

[37]Laracy, "The Catholic Mission," in Friendly Islands,
139. "The Wesleyan mission was established in Savai'i in
1828 by a Samoan who had been converted in Tonga. Several
Tongan Wesleyan teachers married to Samoans were also known
to be residing on Savai'i around 1828...." Sharon Tiffany,
"Politics of Denominational Organization," in Mission,
Church, and Sect in Oceania, 427.

See also Tippett, People Movements...., 112.

[38]Macdonald, Cinderellas of the Empire, 40.

[39]Ibid., 41. Macdonald notes that Funafuti may have
come under the influence of Rotuman converts who drifted to
the island.

[40]Much of the material in this passage was drawn from
Macdonald's excellent study of Gilbert and Ellice Islands'
history, Cinderellas of the Empire. See 38.

[41]Ibid., 50.

[42]Wiltgen, The Founding of the Roman Catholic Church in
Oceania, 159.

[43]Ibid., 344.

[44]Clearly there was a case of circular causation
involved here as well.

[45]Maude, Of Islands and Men, 163.

[46]Maude notes that "a few Europeans did reach and survive for a time in Melanesia," 145. Twenty castaways on
Malaita in 1829 appear to have been kept alive so that they
might be devoured during pagan festivals. Maude concludes
that Melanesia and New Guinea were "scarcely a propitious
home for beachcombers during the early part of the century,
and even the convicts apparently by-passed the area." 146.

[47]Eastern Polynesia was subject to the impact of the Peruvian labor trade in 1862-1863 but by this time all of the major island groups had been subject to missionary attention.

[48]Peter Corris, Passage, Port and Plantation: A History of Solomon Islands Labour Migration 1870-1914, [Melbourne: Melbourne University Press, 1973]. See 121-124.

[49]Gilson, Cook Islands, 31. Referring to Polynesia in general, Garrett notes that "receptiveness to the new religion sprang from readiness to believe that the God of the newcomers, like the ships, must be more powerful than their own."

[50]Ibid., 6

[51]Gilson, Cook Islands, 31.

[52]As quoted in Tiffany, "Politics of Denominational Organization," in Mission, Church, and Sect in Oceania, 424.

[53]See Tippett, People Movements in Southern Polynesia, 147-170; "Cultural Determinants and the Acceptance of Christianity: An Anthropological Analysis of the Case of Samoa."

[54]Tiffany, "Politics of Denominational Organization," in Mission, Church, and Sect in Oceania, 424.

[55]Ibid.

[56]Ibid.

[57]Ibid., 432.

[58]As quoted in ibid., 424.

[59]Macdonald, Cinderellas of the Empire, 43.

[60]For a discussion of the factors effecting "rapid Christianisation" in the Cooks, see Gilson, Cook Islands, 23.

[61]Garrett, "The Conflict ... Samoa," The Journal of Pacific History, 9 (1974), 67.

[62]Latukefu, "The Wesleyan Mission," in Friendly Islands, 117. When the Wesleyan missionaries, Thomas and Hutchinson, arrived in Tonga, the chief of Hihifo, Ata, gave them land but refused to accept Christianity and forbade his people to do so.

[63]As Garrett observed: "British misconceptions about
the power of the Pomare line on Tahiti proved to be one of
the mission's gravest problems for the first eighteen years
of its work." Garrett, To Live Among the Stars, 8.

[64]Ibid.

[65]As quoted in Newbury, Tahiti Nui, 32.

[66]Ibid., 27.

[67]Ibid., p. 38 and Gilson, Cook Islands, 21.

[68]Latukefu, "The Wesleyan Mission," in Friendly Islands,
120.

[69]Ibid., 125.

[70]Ibid.

[71]Latukefu, "The Wesleyan Mission," in Friendly Island,
117. This passage refers to Tonga.

[72]Gilson, Cook Islands, 21.

[73]Macdonald, Cinderellas of the Empire, 43.

[74]Garrett, To Live Among the Stars, 11.

[75]Ibid.

[76]Ibid., 12.

[77]Ibid., 13.

[78]Osterwal, "Introduction," in Mission, Church and Sect
in Oceania, 32.

[79]As quoted in Macdonald, Cinderellas of the Empire,
39.

[80]Ibid.

[81]Ibid., 52.

[82]Hilliard, God's Gentlemen, 3.

[83]Ibid., 23.

[84]Ibid., 22.

[85]Gilson, Cook Islands, 25.

[86]Newbury, Tahiti Nui, 36.

[87]Garrett, To Live Among the Stars, 19.

[88]Ibid., 19.

[89]As quoted in Newbury, Tahiti Nui, 36.

[90]Latukefu, "The Wesleyan Mission" in Friendly Islands, 124.

[91]Laracy, "The Catholic Mission", in Friendly Islands, 140.

[92]Ibid., 136.

[93]Ibid.

[94]Wiltgen, The Founding of the Roman Catholic Church in Oceania, 231.

[95]Ibid., 472.

[96]David Hilliard, "Colonialism and Christianity: The Melanesian Mission in the Solomon Islands," The Journal of Pacific History, 9 (1974), 97.

[97]Ibid., 98; See also John Bach, "The Royal Navy in the Pacific Islands," The Journal of Pacific History, 3 (1968), 3-20.

[98]Hilliard, "Colonialism and Christianity...," The Journal of Pacific History, 9 (1974), 97.

[99]Wiltgen, The Founding of the Roman Catholic Church in Oceania, 471.

[100]Hilliard, "Colonialism and Christianity...," The Journal of Pacific History, 9 (1974), 99; Navies were not always prepared to help missionaries as fully as the missionaries might have liked. See, for example, Laracy, "The Catholic Mission," in Friendly Islands, 144.

[101]Latukefu, "The Impact of South Sea Islands Missionaries on Melanesia," in Mission, Church, and Sect in Oceania, 91.

[102]Another almost insuperable obstacle was the Roman
Catholic expectation of celibacy. Interestingly, while
other missions benefited from using island teachers, the
Sacred Heart Mission benefited from restricting the use of
Gilbertese pastors since the Gilbertese considered Pacific
Islands teachers as second best. See Macdonald, Cinderellas
of the Empire, 51.

[103]Gilson, Cook Islands, 21.

[104]Ibid., 22.

[105]Macdonald, Cinderellas of the Empire, 39.

[106]Ibid., 31.

[107]Gilson, Cook Islands, 107.

[108]Latukefu, "The Impact of South Sea Islands
Missionaries on Melanesia," in Mission, Church, and Sect in
Oceania, 98.

[109]Bishop Selwyn of the Melanesian Mission maintained
that "Nature, by dividing the Pacific into separate islands
and archipelagos had 'marked out for each missionary body
its field of duty.' Wasteful competition and sectarian
controversy could thus in principle be avoided." Hilliard,
God's Gentlemen, 7.

[110]Laracy, "The Catholic Mission," in Friendly Islands,
138; As Laracy points out (137): "One of the first books
published by the Wesleyans in Fiji was a denunciation of
'Lotu Popi' which appeared in 1839, less than two years after
the Marists arrived in Western Polynesia."

[111]Latukefu, "The Wesleyan Mission," in Friendly Islands,
134.

[112]Macdonald, Cinderellas of the Empire, 50.

[113]Tiffany, "Politics of Denominational Organization," in
Mission, Church, and Sect in Oceania, 430.

[114]Macdonald, Cinderellas of the Empire, 38.

[115]Latukefu, "The Impact of South Sea Islands
Missionaries on Melanesia," in Mission, Church, and Sect in
Oceania, 99; In extreme cases, Latukefu notes, racist over-
tones were quite overt. He cites the example of a Tongan
missionary and his wife who were invited to the mission
house for tea but were told to bring their own cups and
saucer (100).

[116]Latukefu, "The Wesleyan Mission," in Friendly Islands, 115.

[117]Hilliard, God's Gentleman, 4.

[118]Gilson, Cook Islands, 41.

[119]Laracy, "The Catholic Mission," in Friendly Islands, 141.

[120]Latukefu, "The Impact of South Sea Islands Missionaries on Melanesia," in Mission, Church, and Sect in Oceania, 92.

[121]Latukefu, "The Wesleyan Mission," in Friendly Islands, 120.

[122]Hilliard, God's Gentlemen, 54.

[123]Ibid.

[124]Ibid., 15.

[125]Ibid., 19.

[126]As quoted in Tiffany, "Politics of Denominational Organization" in Mission, Church, and Sect in Oceania, 429.

[127]As quoted in Wiltgen, The Founding of the Catholic Church in Oceania, 473; Verguet concluded "Mission work, therefore, is very difficult and perilous in these barbaric countries."

[128]Latukefu, "The Wesleyan Missiion," in Friendly Islands, 115; A similar relationship between trade goods and conversion obtained in Samoa. "The alacrity with which [LMS] missionaries and teachers were accepted, and with which at least nominal conversions took place," Tiffany writes, "was associated with the desire to obtain foreign goods which the missionaries seemed capable of dispensing." Tiffany, "Politics of Denominational Organization in Samoa," in Mission, Church, and Sect in Oceania, 429.

[129]Hilliard, God's Gentlemen, 82.

[130]As quoted in ibid.

[131]Macdonald, Cinderellas of the Empire, 52.

[132]As quoted in ibid.

[133]Latukefu, "The Wesleyan Mission," in Friendly
Islands, 122.

[134]Hilliard, God's Gentlemen, 34; Hilliard also makes
some interesting observations about the relationship between
the linguistic capabilities of the various heads of mission
and instructional policy.

[135]As quoted in Macdonald, Cinderellas of the Empire,
33; After Bingham had collected 2000 words on his own he
paid a young convert a dollar for each additional one
hundred words the latter could provide.

[136]Latukefu, "The Wesleyan Mission," in Friendly
Islands, 123.

[137]Macdonald, Cinderellas of the Empire, 33.

[138]Ibid., 35.

[139]Latukefu, "The Wesleyan Mission," in Friendly
Islands, 123.

[140]As quoted in Tiffany, "Politics of Denominational
Organization in Samoa," in Mission, Church, and Sect in
Oceania, 430.

[141]Latukefu, "The Wesleyan Mission," in Friendly
Islands, 124.

[142]Ibid., 129.

[143]Latukefu, "The Impact of South Sea Islands
Missionaries on Melanesia," in Mission, Church, and Sect in
Oceania, 97.

[144]Wiltgen, The Founding of the Roman Catholic Church
in Oceania, 468. Another excellent study, unpublished so
far as this author knows, is Hugh Laracy's "Roman Catholic
Martyrs in the South Pacific, 1841-1855."

[145]Wiltgen, The Founding of the Roman Catholic Church
in Oceania, 468.

[146]Ibid., 332.

[147]Ibid., 475. The Melanesian Mission suffered a similar grievous loss with the death of Bishop Patteson at the
hands of Nukapuans in 1871. However, his death did not come
during an initial conversion phase and it is somewhat difficult to assess the real impact of his murder on the Mission's
continuing program of conversion.

[148]Gilson, Cook Islands, 33.

[149]Tiffany, "Politics of Denominational Organization," in Mission, Church, and Sect in Oceania, 428.

CHAR MILLER

DOMESTICITY ABROAD:

WORK AND FAMILY IN THE SANDWICH ISLAND MISSION, 1820-1840

"Of all the trials incident to missionary life, the responsibility of training up children . . . is the only one worth being named."

Lucy Thurston

Levi Bingham's birth was much heralded. Born on New Year's Day, his parents, Hiram and Sybil Bingham, pioneer missionaries to Hawaii, hoped that their first son would help usher in a new era in the Islands, that his arrival would prove "the harbinger of peace to the mission." In naming him after Levi Parsons, a friend of the family and a missionary who had recently given his life to the Lord's cause in the Middle East, they expected that the peace the child would bring would be that of a Christian missionary: Their wish was that he "be one among the many whom God will raise up to fill in some important sense...heavenly plans."[1]

That heaven itself figured in those plans was not quite what Hiram and Sybil Bingham had envisioned. Less than three weeks after his birth, Levi Bingham--as had his namesake--died in mission service. In death, as in his short life, the child had a public role to play. His burial was the first in the mission's brief history, and, as a result, his parents and their colleagues used the opportunity to further the Lord's case before the Hawaiian people. "The king and principle chiefs and distinguished women" of the Islands were invited to the funeral, which was

designed to display the solemnity and decorous nature of
true Christian burials. It was, all in the mission agreed,
a sharp (and welcome) contrast to the explosive, often
riotous, grief that marked the deaths of Hawaiian royalty.
The missionaries hoped that the Islanders would absorb the
lesson Levi's death offered and begin to practice Christian
customs.   If they did so, then Levi Bingham's death would
indeed have fulfilled "heavenly plans."[2]

The circumstances surrounding Levi's death revealed the
extent to which the Bingham family's grief formed a part of
the mission's work.   They were not, of course, the only
missionaries to learn how profoundly intertwined issues of
work and family could be. This interconnection lay at the
core of the missionary experience, as the American
missionaries to Hawaii and later to Micronesia, and the
English missionaries in the South Pacific, came to
recognize. And there was a reason for the centrality: The
English and American mission boards believed that in general
Christian families-- not individual missionaries--were the
most effective means of inculcating Christian values and
beliefs abroad; since the nuclear family was considered a
key component of western civilization and culture, it was
through that form that the blessings of Christianity would
best flow. A missionary's public role and private life were
deliberately linked, for the mission boards believed that
this interconnection would sustain the missionary in time of
need, provide immunization against sexual temptation and
enable potential converts to witness how true Christians
lived and worked.[3]

That at least was the theory that emerged from discussions within the American Board of Commissioners for Foreign
Missions (ABCFM), the major force behind American mission
work, when, following the War of 1812, it decided to launch
its evangelical crusade throughout the world. And it is
this context which makes the Sandwich Island Mission, the

first American mission to the Pacific, so important. It was
to serve as a test case of the strength and effectiveness of
the Christian crusade in that region, especially of the
contribution of missionary families to that cause. This
primacy and emphasis meant that everything that the Sandwich
Island Mission did would set precedent for future American
missions in the Pacific (and elsewhere)--and nowhere was
this more true than in the the arena of work and family
relations. By exploring this interconnection, then, one can
gain a deeper sense of the texture of the missionaries'
lives, of their perceptions of their work, and of the image
of themselves that they hoped to project, issues of great
importance to a fledgling mission.[4]

These issues are important in another respect, for they
illuminate questions of growing scholarly concern: To what
degree does work shape the conditions of family life, and to
what extent does the reverse hold true? Until recently,
scholars from a variety of disciplines have focused only on
the first question, assuming that economic and social forces
outside the home have largely determined the course of life
within it; the family is usually seen as a dependent
variable, an assessment that presumably has held true over
time and across cultures. But increasingly this notion is
being challenged. Increasingly historians, sociologists and
others are exploring the ways familial concerns influence
(if not significantly set) the conditions for work. As
historian Tamara Hareven has pointed out, the family can
operate as an independent variable--in her words, as an
"active agent"--and thereby influence the context in which
members work. But, Hareven cautions, being "an active or
passive agent does not imply that the family was in full
control of its destiny" and she therefore argues that "the
crucial historical question is...rather under what
historical conditions was it able to control its environment
and under what circumstances did its control diminish?"[5]

The experience of the Sandwich Island missionaries
fully underscores the complexity of Hareven's argument.
Their lives reveal, on the one hand, that family life was
not simply dependent on work for its character: The
Christian missionaries' vision of the private (and nuclear)
family, for example, clearly influenced the way the men and
women of the mission sought to convert the Hawaiians.   Yet
it is just as clear that the particular circumstances in
which the missionaries labored altered the familial context,
alterations that had significant personal and professional
ramifications.   This is important for it suggests that the
Hawaiians helped shape the context of mission work.   They
did so in the public arena by determining when and to what
extent to convert to Christianity.   But they also influenced
--if more subtly--private life within the mission compound.
They were in a sense the audience for whom the American
missionaries performed, thereby setting the stage for,
giving meaning to, and defining the course of much of the
cross cultural dialogue that ensued.   There was, in short, a
dynamic reciprocity between work and family that formed such
a critical element in the lives of the New England missionaries in the Pacific.   There was, in short, a reciprocal
process at work, one that formed a critical element in the
lives of the New England missionaries in the Pacific.

Questions concerning the interaction between mission
work and family life arose even before the missionaries
sailed from Boston to Hawaii in October 1819.   Not all
supporters of the missionary movement were convinced, as was
the ABCFM leadership, that it was appropriate (and
necessary) to send married couples to raise the Lord's
banner in foreign lands.   To meet this challenge, the ABCFM

arranged a series of public ceremonies at each step of the mission's formation--at the ordination of its two mission- aries, Hiram Bingham and Asa Thurston, in September, at these two men's respective weddings several weeks later and at a final religious service just before the mission sailed- -during which sermons were delivered stressing the prominent role missionary family life would play in Christianizing the Hawaiians. To those who reproached the women who chose to go to the Islands, the Rev. Thomas Gallaudet, who officiated at the wedding of Hiram Bingham and Sybil Moseley, responded that all Protestants should feel "grateful...to those willing to take their lives in their hands...[and], in some measure, to fulfill our obligation to our Saviour." The women's devotion and piety, he continued, had an additional ramification: It would strengthen the resolve of the male missionary. Was not woman, he asked, "sent by Heaven as a helpmate for man; designed to share and soothe his sorrows; to participate in and lighten his cares[?]" If so, then missionary women, because of their strength, would at times "invigorate" their missionary husbands' "languishing efforts in the path of duty," or extricate the mission "from difficulties which his boasted sagacity cannot surmount," all the while, "like the vestal virgin of old, keeping bright the light of domestic piety." The women, in short, would prod their husbands onward, contributing to and standing as a symbol of all that their husbands hoped to accomplish in the Islands.[6]

Gallaudet's argument was deeply imbued with the antebellum American concept of domesticity, which imputed particular moral strengths and religious virtues to women, traits that reportedly arose out of their nurturant and maternal characters. Yet Gallaudet's emphasis upon domesticity did not mean that he (and, by extension, the ABCFM) supposed that the women missionaries' only value lay

within the mission home; there was more to it than that.   It
was   these   women's   special   mission,   the   Rev.   Samuel
Worcester, secretary of the ABCFM, declared: "To shew to the
rude and depraved Islanders an effective example of the
purity   and   dignity   and   loveliness--the   salutary   and
vivifying   influence--,   the   attractive   and   celestial
excellence, which Christianity can impart to the female
character."   To fulfill that obligation, the women must go
beyond the mission's walls, and enter Hawaiian society (and
homes)   to   "inculcate   conjugal   fidelity   and   domestic
attachment, parental care and filial obedience" as well as
"to educate the rising generation [and] to ameliorate the
condition of the female sex."   The women in the Sandwich
Island Mission were to play an active and public role in the
reformation of Hawaiian society.[7]

          Gallaudet and Worcester neatly fit their arguments to
their culture's   prescription for women's proper sphere of
activity, and yet managed to justify the ABCFM's conviction
that missionary families must form the core of the Christian
crusade, a conviction that perforce stretched the boundaries
of that sphere.   Their arguments nonetheless quieted the
critics, stilling what one friend of the mission described
as "the barking of little dogs."   But what these men could
not   forsee   was   the   disquiet   that   emerged   from   the
exportation of domesticity and from the notion that members
of the mission--especially the women--had public and private
roles to play, both of which were critical to the mission's
success.   On occasion, this engendered tensions that the
women and the men of the mission could not easily resolve or
reconcile.[8]

          But, at first, all seemed propitious.   When the
missionaries reached the Islands in the Spring of 1820, they
were cheered to learn that the tapus had been broken, that
the fabric of Hawaiian society and religion was beginning to

unravel, a situation they expected would increase their prospects for success. Here they were particularly intrigued by what this meant for the missionary women. "Jehovah cast down the idols of the heathens of this land," one male missionary wrote, "and actually prepared the way for our female helpers to be well received, and to be treated with much kindness and to be made extremely useful." One use in particular was that the women's presence indicated the mission's "Pacific design" and insured that "the blessings of civilization [will] be imparted and the privileges of Christian religion secured to this people much earlier than could be done without them."[9]

Women may have accelerated the processes of conversion, but Hawaii did not represent a speedy victory for the forces of Christ. As with other missionaries in the Pacific, the American missionaries in Hawaii found that their inadequate knowledge of the culture in which they were working hampered, often undermined, their efforts. They assumed, for example, that the breaking of the tapus shattered the people's allegiance to traditional forms of worship, an assumption that badly underestimated the Hawaiians' gods' resilience and lulled the missionaries into a false sense of the inevitability of the Christian conquest. Inadequate too was their understanding of the vital role women played in Hawaiian culture and politics. Reared in a society in which women and men operated in separate spheres, in which domesticity defined--some say circumscribed--women's activities, the American missionaries at first ignored the significant positions held by and the respect granted to women of royal blood.[10]

As important as these and other misconceptions were in determining the speed and scope of the mission's success during the initial period of contact, there was another factor, one that especially shaped the influence that the

American women were able to exert in the missionary cause.
Upon their arrival in the Islands, they were immediately
confronted with the conflict imbedded in their assigned
positions as both public and private figures; to be fully
active in mission work outside the home and be exemplars of
domestic virtue within it, was impossible. This was largely
due to the mounting chores the women assumed within the
mission family, chores that were particularly onerous at the
Honolulu station. In a letter to her sisters, Sybil Bingam
outlined the the tasks she confronted during one arduous
period in the Summer and early Fall of 1822. The mission
family in Honolulu, she wrote, comprised four "distinct
families, united in one, all having children--all having
infants, with eighteen or twenty native children divided
among them, two native youths, Thomas and Nonorei, and one
young man, Mr. Harwood, from New England." This assembly
was crammed into "one frame house, containing five rooms, 12
ft. by 12 ft. above and below...with a stone room and eating
room on the ground cellar." Not all of these rooms,
however, were designed for the inhabitants' exclusive use:
One " was considered as necessary for common resort,"
leaving four "in which to place the beds of eight parents
and their little ones, and accommodate the gentlemen, two of
the three desiring separate beds." Things only got worse
when several other missionaries arrived for a visit, at
which point the Binghams (and their child) moved up into the
"upper half story" of the house. "The roof was low," Sybil
reported, "but a field bedstead could stand," and with two
trunks serving as chairs, this small, cramped space was
their home for many months. The shortage of space forced
all in the mission to show "patience and prudence, to
sustain the character of good neighbors."[11]

      Personality conflicts were the least of Sybil Bingham's
worries, however. "Ways and means must be devised," she

wrote, "and labor done that so many might be fed, each day, with food convenient for them." That was no small task, especially as most of the women at the station were already weary. For awhile "Mrs. Loomis superintended the domestic concerns, though hardly able to keep about, from the great exertion she had made...Mrs. C[hamberlain], having care of the washing and ironing...with the daily charge of the visiting gentlemen--her husband feeble--one or two children ill...felt it difficult to take care of the cellar kitchen." Soon thereafter "Mrs. L. gave up and took to her bed. Mrs. C. felt it her duty, rather than mine, to take the place below," Sybil Bingham continued, but in time she too withdrew when her husband "had a most violent attack of rheumatism and required her whole attention." Sybil, who had been caring for the children and teaching school, felt she had no alternative--she closed her school for several months and "went below--stood at the helm, and except [for] a few of the first days of my labor, had the care of seeing that 50 were fed with something, three times a day." That regimen took its toll on Sybil, too, and when her health failed, the women reluctantly asked Mr. Harwood, their guest from New England, to tend to the kitchen until one of the women was healthy enough to relieve him.[12]

This continuous and time-consuming work had many ramifications. The women's response to these burdens, for example, was not to ask their husbands for relief; to have done so would have been to draw them away from true missionary endeavors. Rather, they sought Hawaiian labor to assume some of their domestic chores. Yet even this reasonable concession caused some to worry that, by hiring others, they were neglecting their own proper duties, thereby diminishing the value of domesticity as an ideal the Hawaiians should absorb. (And when critics of the mission in the U.S. and Hawaii charged that the missionary women lived off the labor of others, the women were doubly chagrined.) But Lucy

Thurston, for one, found such concerns wrongheaded. She
made it a point to advise all those women who came to Hawaii
after the first generation of missionaries "that to live a
holy life is one thing, and to sap one's constitution in the
ardor of youthful feelings is quite another." The
experiences of Lucy Thurston, Sybil Bingham and the others
made one thing clear: "Do not be devoted to domestic
duties. Trust to natives." If they did not do so, their
health would fail and their ability to contribute to the
cause would be, perforce, limited.[13]

Their health failed in any event. As Hiram Bingham
advised the ABCFM, "most of the females of the mission
suffer materially from debility which is in part attributed
to the climate and in part to the hardships and privations
they have suffered," an assessment with which Laura Judd
would have agreed: "My constitution suffers from the
continual debilitating effects of a tropical climate," she
wrote a friend: "I feel the need of bracing winters." Others
felt similarly, sought out those winters, and left the
missionary field for the United States. For those who
stayed, the struggle continued. "My own dear wife has been
confined to the couch about 20 days with alarming symptoms
of a broken constitution," Hiram Bingham reported in late
1825. "She has been ill about three months and is now lower
than Mrs. Stewart or any other member of the mission," an
observation that reveals the general state of the mission's
health as well. Bingham's only hope was that the Lord "will
raise [Sybil] up again and enable her to bear her equal part
with her husband in winning the nation to Christ."[14]

His was a vain hope, and none knew that better than his
wife. She and the other women recognized that the increase
in domestic labor and the decline in physical health
restricted their direct contributions to the mission cause.
At best, they were able to shape their mission work around

the needs of their families. "My mornings are devoted to
the cares of my family," Laura Judd declared, "and I am
ambitious to be an exemplary wife and mother and housekeeper
so that my husband may be known when he sits among the
elders of the land." In this way she would at least have an
indirect influence on the mission's success. When possible,
usually during the afternoons, she was able more directly to
shape events, by teaching "native schools" or "from time to
time to meet with a circle of females...to read and explain
the scriptures." But even such a limited schedule was hard
to maintain. Illnesses intervened—"when my health will
permit," Charlotte Baldwin allowed, "I meet with different
classes three afternoons a week," but her health was
unsteady, so her schedule was upset. Family cares intruded
as well. As Lucy Thurston observed, only that time which
she could "redeem" from her family (which was not much)
could she give to the Hawaiians. In short, most found, as
did Sybil Bingham, that "time seems...divided into little
parcels" and "the days and hours...filled with little, busy
cares." As a result there was little question of the
missionary women playing what Hiram Bingham had visualized
as an "equal part" in the Christian crusade. They simply
did not have the time.[15]

No wonder that a tone of frustration occasionally crept
into the women's letters and diaries. Exhausted by domestic
cares, they could rarely participate in the grand
reformation of Hawaii that had drawn them there in the first
place. "I sometimes grieve," one confided, "that I can no
more devote myself to the language and the study of the
Bible," two activities that not only characterized male
missionary work but ones which were necessary for effective
proselytizing. Her grief, however, was checked in two ways.
Her devotion, and the larger theological framework in which
she and all missionaries operated, explained her situation

and brought solace: "I believe that God appoints my work; it is enough for me to see that I do it all with an eye to his glory." And there was consolation too in a more secular way: "I am allowed to aid one whose constant employment is in the way of direct efforts for [the Hawaiians'] good." By indicating that only male missionaries could be constantly and directly engaged in the Lord's work, by acknowledging, as another put it, that "the missionary best serves his generation who serves the public and his wife best serves her generation who serves her family," the women of the Sandwich Island Mission conformed nicely with Rev. Thomas Gallaudet's vision of the "heaven-sent helpmate." But they also acknowledged that they could not consistently meet that other expectation of them, that they be active, public figures.[16]

The dilemmas of missionary womanhood were intensified by those of missionary parenthood. The children of the mission once more brought into focus the inescapable interconnection of work and family. Their births, of course, brought great joy to their parents, but created yet another public responsibility. "Our patrons expect, the world expects, the heathen themselves expect, that [the children] will rise up and reflect honor upon an enlightened origin," one missionary mother wrote. To so reflect, the children from birth were to lead emblematic lives, a point made clear in the death of Levi Bingham and in the infancy of other mission children. To help the mission secure royal favor, for example, Sybil Bingham and Maria Whitney visited Liholiho and members of the royal family in 1822. "We would by all means win their favor and confidence if we could," Sybil Bingham indicated, so "sister Maria and I took our sweet babes that they might plead for us." That one of these sweet babes was a matter of weeks old, indicated how soon the children took on public personas.[17]

Infants were one thing, but full-fledged children were
another, posing as they did major questions concerning
missionary childrearing practices. Was it possible, the
missionary parents wondered, to raise dutiful Christian
children in a land they considered savage and "polluted"?
The stakes were high and the situation complex: If the
children stayed with their parents, they ran the risk of
being "corrupted" by the surrounding culture, and should
that occur (and most felt certain that it would), then the
mission's image of Christian decorum and familial piety
would be forever tarnished in Hawaii and in the United
States. No less worrisome were the possible results of
sending the children back to the U.S. for education: If the
mission parents did this, they might offend the domestic
Christian public's attachment to the concept of domesticity
which made glorious the mother-child bond. Finally, if the
children were sent to the U.S., they (and their families)
could not serve as role models in Hawaii. The mission
family struggled with this complicated issue for twenty
years, a struggle that consumed much of its time. The
struggle also revealed the shadowy but significant role the
Hawaiians played in mission life and highlighted an
important difference in parents' perceptions of the purposes
and principles of missionary service, issues that
significantly shaped the content of that service.[18]

The first test case was not one to lift the hearts of
the Sandwich Island Mission family. Indeed, the situation
surrounding the Chamberlain family served as a warning to
all of the dangers associated with children on missionary
ground. Daniel and Jerusha Chamberlain had sailed with the
Binghams, Thurstons and the others in 1819, but unlike their
peers in the pioneer company, they brought five children
with them to Hawaii. Their children ranged in age from two
to thirteen, and their ages proved a problem. Willing and

able to range beyond the mission compound, beyond
supervision, they came into contact on a regular basis with
the Hawaiians, with what one missionary called "this rude
people, where delicacy is scarcely known or thought of."
This "contaminating intercourse" apparently began to leave
its mark, and the Chamberlains and the other missionaries
labored "long and hard to give [the] children suitable
instruction and to watch over them." This solicitude in the
end was ineffective, for, the missionaries agreed, Hawaii of
the early 1820s lacked "the firmness of Christian
discipline" which would reinforce Christian parents'
concerns. As it was, there was little the mission could
then do to prevent the Chamberlain children (or any other)
from "coming into close contact with the natives." The only
solution available was for the Chamberlains to leave the
Islands, a decision that was strongly supported by a
visiting deputation of English missionaries from Tahiti,
where similar problems with missionary offspring had been
faced and a similar decision reached; the missionaries'
negative perceptions of the Hawaiians' influence on the
American children suggest how the Islanders helped determine
the life course of the mission family.[19]

This decision was not without its problems, however.
The mission recognized that it might be some time before
Hawaii adopted "the firmness of Christian discipline," which
meant that during the interim many, if not all, of the
missionary children (and possibly their parents) would have
to leave the Islands. Not only would the ABCFM and its
domestic supporters disapprove of this policy--for if all
left, how would the mission continue?--but the absence of
completed families among the missionaries might extend the
period required to bring about the evangelization they so
desired. Taken by itself, the Chamberlain family's
experience offered little solace.

The first generation of missionaries nonetheless had to
come to terms with this issue, though they were not united
in the resolutions they reached. Two responses emerged,
responses that, in part, were determined by the
missionaries' geographic locale and by how the particular
families viewed their role in the mission. Those in
Honolulu, for example, strongly favored sending the
children--generally without parents--back to the mainland.
Aware that this decision challenged accepted views of
childrearing and challenged too the mission's purported
commitment to domesticity, the missionaries on Oahu argued
that theirs was not a normal situation and that they should
not be judged by standards applied in America. They were,
after all, living in Honolulu, a place filled with
boisterous foreigners, innumerable grog shops and other dens
of iniquity. Hardly a spiritual place, Honolulu was also
dangerous, and the parents especially feared for their
children's physical safety and psychological security.
"Their nursery is as it were on the field of battle," Hiram
Bingham wrote the ABCFM in 1828 shortly after sending his
daughter Sophia back to the United States. "We fled with
[her] from the war on Kauai; we carried her asleep into Mr.
Richard's cellar when Lahaina was fired on--but we could not
easily hush her cries, when I and my house were mob'd at
Honolulu nor will she soon lose the impression that we are
here in continual danger from the assaults of wicked men."
The nature and locale of Sophia's parents' work shaped her
childhood in another way, too. There were few other
missionary children near enough to be her companions (at the
time of her departure she had a sister six years younger)
and none outside the mission who were acceptable to her
parents; they were not about to repeat the Chamberlain's
experience. Sophia--and her case was typical--"had no
school, no society suited to her age," a situation from
which her parents thought her "likely to suffer more and

more" as time passed. At least in the United States, where
Sophia would be among friends and family, she would be safe
and not so "emphatically alone."[20]

Nor were the Binghams alone in making this difficult
decision to send a child home. The exodus began slowly in
the late 1820s as those children born earlier in the decade
reached that age--somewhere between eight and twelve--when
their parents feared the consequences of their continued
residence among the Islanders; children from the Ruggles,
Whitney, Bishop and Richard families followed Sophia Bingham
to America. The trickle of departures turned into a flood
by the middle of the next decade; in 1834 alone, for
example, nine children were expected to leave for the
mainland. Five years later, on the twentieth anniversary of
the mission, the total number of departed children was large
indeed. According to Lucy Thurston, "more than forty
missionaries' children have been conveyed away by parents,
that have retired from this field of labor. Eighteen have
been scattered about in the fatherland without parents."
These figures reflect the pervasiveness of the problem and
suggest that few, if any, of the mission families were
untouched by it. Moreover, these numbers suggest too that
the need for continual reinforcements of the mission from
the United States was not simply a result of the
missionaries' success in spreading Christ's message, but due
to the mission's failure to solve the critical issue of
childrearing.[21]

Concern for the missionary children's future was not
the only reason so many were sent away. Some parents did so
to lessen their parental obligations so that they might more
effectively fulfill their obligation to the Lord. It was,
one wrote, a question of balance: children helped to sap
their parents' strength, vigor that might be best expended
on the "thousands of another language [who] are looking to

them for attention, care and instruction." The missionary's
first duty, then, lay with those they had come to convert;
as Samuel Whitney, a father of four, commented, "If I had
not sent away my children, 1835 would not find me at the
Sandwich Islands." The missionary women's first duty also
lay with the Hawaiians, or so Hiram Bingham advocated: "The
theory that it is the duty of a missionary <u>mother</u> to guide,
watch over and educate her children, whatever else she may
do or fail to do," required some revision. Fathers and
mothers "are jointly bound to provide for their children,
and train them up for Christ and heaven," he declared, "but
not necessarily under the same roof." The missionary mother
"who is qualified to give her own offspring a thorough
education on missionary ground...is, or ought to be,
qualified to teach a multitude of those whose mothers cannot
teach them well at all." As such, it made more sense (and
possibly more converts) for the missionary mother "to
instruct the multitude...while...the missionary child is
committed to the hands of others, either on missionary
ground or far over the sea."[22]

    This pragmatic asssessment had its emotional costs.
"To turn our little ones from us," Sybil Bingham wrote,
"sometimes literally forcing them from our arms as we embark
them upon the wide waters" was painful. Ironically, some of
that pain was eased by the support given to the mission
policy by the very Hawaiians whose characters assemed to
warrant breaking up mission families. For instance,
Kaahumanu, <u>Kuhina</u> <u>nui</u>, or executive officer of Hawaii,
agreed with the missionaries that hers were a "depraved
people." Her words not only gave her an active voice in
determining the mission's course of action but also
sanctified it: The missionary women used her assessment in
their letters home to justify a decision they knew would not
be well received. Such justification, of course, could not

fully quell parental "apprehensions for the rocks and shoals
that [lay] in their [children's] course." Sending his
daughter Sophia to the United States was a "severe
struggle," Hiram Bingham acknowledged, "and the path has
never...been sufficiently marked to induce us to walk in it
without shrinking." Yet walk in it he did, and, once having
made the decision, Bingham was "comforted . . . in the
reflection that we have done . . . for what the good of the
child and the cause of the mission required." In so saying,
he spoke for many who--even with heavy hearts--believed that
mission work set the conditions for family life.[23]

He did not speak for all, however. A minority
believed--and acted on the belief--that the needs of the
mission family shaped the work environment. This group
probably included some of those who resigned from their
positions and left the Islands with their families,
unwilling as they may have been to separate from their
children. And it certainly included Lucy Thurston who
sharply disagreed (and made her disagreement public) with
the approach those in Honolulu took on this issue. "To send
away children at an age so early, while I am sustained in
active life, is what every feeling in my heart revolts
against," she declared, a declaration that indicates that
she was more willing than some to reduce significantly her
missionary endeavors for the sake of her children. Her
husband, she explained, was "entirely devoted to works of a
public nature. My duties are of a more private character,"
a division of labor with which she was happy. Nor did she
feel "like some of our mothers, that children must be sent
away or ruined. I harp upon another string, and say, make
better provision for them, or [ruination] will be the likely
result."[24]

The provisions she made to prevent the ruination of her
children revolved around the physical layout of her mission
home. Her general principle, she advised a cousin who was

establishing a mission in Turkey, was that "houses and
dooryards must be laid out to meet the character of the
people and the exigencies of the times." Both demanded that
missionaries protect themselves, and, although missionaries
are "public characters and their houses...public houses,"
this did not mean that the entire house need be open to the
public. Privacy must be maintained, and the way to do this
was to create an architecture that both showcased the family
and separated it from the non-Christians, one that revealed
the family's purity and kept it pure.[25]

The ideal home for the "pioneer missionary," Lucy
Thurston wrote, would "consist of three distinct
departments, so closely connected, that one lady could
superintend them all. One department would be for children,
one for household natives, and one for native company." This
structure made the house at once accessible and defensible:
It let "each class know its place," she commented, "and the
whole [would] move on without collision." Determined to
order the family's life and its interactions with the
Hawaiians along such ideal lines, Lucy and Asa Thurston so
constructed their home at Kailua on the island of Hawaii.
Set behind and above the village on an "arid slope," the
Thurston homestead of five acres was entirely "enclosed with
a stone wall three feet wide and six feet high, with simply
the front gate for entrance." From that gate to "each side
of the front door" ran two walls parallel to the walkway,
effectively sealing off the adjacent yards. Similar
partitioning, shaped by the family's needs, occurred within
the house. There were public reception rooms from which one
could enter the front yard designed for Hawaiian visitors.
Other rooms (and yards) were off-limits to all but the
immediate family--the Hawaiians "know precisely where to
enter the yard and the house, and they have learned where to
stop"--but on the off-chance that they did not, there was

only one door that led to the Thurston's rooms and to its
separate backyard. And at that door stood Lucy Thurston:
"If I am entertaining company in the sitting room [I can
remain]...devoted to the natives [but] still [be] porter to
the only door that leads into the children's special
enclosure, and have the satisfied feeling of their being
safe, beyond the reach of native influence." Islander
influence was more pervasive than Thurston thought, however.
The very erection of such elaborate architectural defenses
indicates how influential the Hawaiians had been in molding
the coutours of mission family life.[26]

Few in the mission were as systematic as the Thurstons
were in developing such an exclusive architecture; those in
Honolulu, for example, erected a fence around the mission
compound to fend off the "moral dearth" around them, but
found it had little impact due to the central location of
the mission in a town significantly larger than Kailua. But
those in Honolulu and the outlying stations justified their
architecture in similar ways, purified children being only
one such justification. The separateness they sought was
justified as well by the sense of mission that the American
missionaries brought with them to the Pacific. The
instructions that the Sandwich Island Mission received from
the Prudential Committee of the ABCFM before leaving the
United States, and which all subsequent missions would
receive, urged them to inculcate both Christianity and
civilization, the two being parts of a whole, a goal that
included alterations in the physical landscape as well.
"Aim at nothing short of covering those islands with
fruitful fields, and pleasant dwellings, and schools and
churches; of raising up the whole people to an educated
state of Christian civilization." The very houses in which
the missionaries lived, and the churches in which they led
prayers, were not only to reflect the mission's presence,

but themselves act as agents of change. Lucy Thurston gave
voice to this when, after a new church was erected in
Kailua, she noted approvingly that it gave "quite an
American look to our village," a look she hoped would
inspire greater piety and decorum. Similarly inspired were
those missionaries who left Hawaii in 1833 to establish a
new (and ill-fated) mission in the Marquesan Islands, where
they constructed a compound designed to radiate moral order
and influence outward among the Marquesans. Although this
particular missionary compound failed in its task (the
Marquesan mission collapsed after less than a year in the
field), Lucy Thurston was convinced that hers had not, that
it helped her meet "the double responsibilities"
missionaries faced--"of molding heathen, and of forming the
characters of our children." Both, she felt, could be
accomplished simultaneously on missionary ground.[27]

Though successful in maintaining separation, the effort
had its drawbacks. "Think of children, cut off from the
benefits of the sanctuary, of schools, of associates," she
wrote, "of children thus exiled I am the mother." That
isolation would only continue, she knew, knowing too that
"when an employment, trade or profession for future life was
chosen, the Sandwich Islands is no longer the place for
them." This acknowlegement that the missionary child's life
cycle determined the make-up of the mission family meant
that it was only a matter of time before Lucy Thurston's
family--the only intact one in the mission--was separated.
In 1839, she and her children sailed from Hawaii, leaving
Asa Thurston behind, a voyage on which she was joined by
Hiram and Sybil Bingham and their remaining children, one
thus marking the end of the pioneer era of the mission.[28]

Its end was marked in other ways too. In the early
1840s, a series of boarding schools for missionary children
were established, schools that increasingly kept the children in the islands, though separated from the Islanders.

Their establishment and growing success suggested that "the firmness of Christian discipline," the lack of which had earlier prompted so many families and children to leave, had reached a sufficient level that the missionary men and women could stay and contribute more fully to a broad range of missionary endeavors. This Americanization came too late for the families of the pioneer generation of the mission. As Lucy Thurston understood, her peers' decision to send children home only seemed "to be introduced to meet the wants of our world, [and are] probably destined only to flourish while the science of missions is in its infancy." One indication that the Sandwich Island Mission had matured was that the particular trials of the pioneer missionary, those deeply rooted in the complex interaction between work and family, no longer formed the core of the missionary experience. They were but part of the mission's past.[29]

NOTES

[1]Hiram Bingham to Jeremiah Evarts, 11 January 1823,
Hawaiian Mission Children's Society (HMCS).

[2]Ibid., See also The Missionary's Daughter: A Memoir of
Lucy Goodale Thurston of the Sandwich Islands, [New York:
The American Tract Society, 1842]; The Mission was pleased
that Levi Bingham's death provided an example for the
Hawaiian royalty to follow, for, six days later, the
"half-sister" of Liholiho died and the King requested a
Christian burial for her, a request that the Missionary
Herald saw as a sign that "the light of the Gospel begins to
shine," and that the "order, the restraint, the decorum of
Christian society" would soon be adopted: MH, October 1823,
318-19. That the Hawaiians might have had motives other
than Christian ones for adopting this form of burial (and
Christianity generally) was not understood. See Dorothy
Barrere and Marshall Sahlins, "Tahitians in the early
history of Hawaiian Christianity: The Journal of Toketa,"
Hawaiian Journal of History, 13 1979, 19-35.

[3]Char Miller, Fathers and Sons: The Bingham Family and
the American Mission, [Philadelphia: Temple University
Press, 1982]; Heman Humphrey, "The Promised Land," [Boston:
Samuel T. Armstrong, 1819]; John Andrew, Rebuilding the
Christian Commonwealth: New England Congregationalists and
Foreign Missions, [Lexington: University Press of Kentucky,
1976]. As Sheldon Dibble, a missionary and one of the
Islands' earliest historians, explained: "The institution
of Christian marriage, lying at the foundation of the family
constitution...had, of course, a very important bearing upon
the social condition, civilization and happiness of the
people." Sheldon Dibble, A History of the Sandwich Islands,
[Honolulu: T. H. Thrum, 1909], 211. See Jane L. Silverman,
"To Marry Again," Hawaiian Journal of History, 17, 1983,
64-75 for a discussion of the ways the missionaries sought
to alter traditional Hawaiian marriage patterns to conform
more closely with New England ones. Although Silverman
notes that monogamous marriages were "quickly adopted by the
alii," she does not explore why the adoption was so swift.
The answer may be that Christianity was a means by which
some of the alii solidified their social and political
power; see K. R. Howe, Where The Waves Fall, [Honolulu:
University of Hawaii Press, 1984].

[4]Humphrey, "The Promised Land," [Boston: Samuel T. Armstrong, 1819]; Andrew, Rebuilding the Christian Commonwealth; Miller, Fathers and Sons.

[5]Tamara Hareven, Family Time and Industrial Time, [New York: Cambridge University Press, 1982], 4; Rossbeth Moss Kanter, Work and Family in the United States: A Critical Review and Agenda for Research and Policy, [New York: Russell Sage Foundation, 1979], 53-58; Ann C. Crouter, "Spillover from Family to Work: The Neglected Side of the Work-Family Interface," presented to the Southeastern Conference on Human Development, Baltimore, Md., April 1982; Hanna Papanek, "Men, Women and Work: Reflections on the Two-Person Career," American Journal of Sociology, 78 (4), 1973, 852-872.

[6]Thomas Gallaudet, "An Address Delivered at a Meeting for Prayer," [Hartford: Lincoln and Stone, 1819], 12.

[7]Carl Degler, At Odds: Women and the Family from the Revolution to the Present, [New York: Oxford University Press, 1980], provides a recent assessment of domesticity and the role it played in shaping women's work, women's sphere. See also Nancy Cott, The Bonds of Womanhood: "Woman's Sphere" in New England, 1780-1835, [New Haven: Yale University Press, 1977]; Barbara Welter, "The Cult of True Womanhood: 1820-1860," American Quarterly, 18 (Summer 1966), 151-174; Samuel Worcester, "Instructions to the Sandwich Island Mission," in Humphrey, "The Promised Land," xii-xiv; Gallaudet, "An Address," 8.

[8]Lucy Thurston, The Life and Times of Lucy Thurston, [Ann Arbor: S. C. Andrews, 1882], 7.

[9]Hiram Bingham to Rev. William Jackson, February 1821, HMCS; M. C. Webb, "The Abolition of the Taboo System in Hawaii," Journal of the Polynesian Society, 74 (1), March 1965, 21-39.

[10]Caroline Ralston, "The Role of the Kamehameha Family in Hawaiian Government," presented to the 94th American Historical Association meetings, December 1979; M. C. Webb, "The Abolition of the Taboo System in Hawaii," 21-39; H. Bingham to Rev. William Jackson, Feb 1821; Miller, Fathers and Sons, Chapter Two.

[11]Sybil Bingham, Diary, 81 (Bingham Family Papers, Yale University Library).

[12]Ibid., 80-81. For a discussion of similar experiences among women missionaries in Papua, see D. Langmore, "A

Neglected Force: White Women Missionaries" in Papua,
1874-1914," Journal of Pacific History, 17 (4), 138-157.

[13]Thurston, Life and Times, 136-137; 130.

[14]Hiram Bingham to Jeremiah Evarts, 18 October 1825,
HMCS; Laura Judd to Lydia Finney, 10 December 1832 in Mary
O'Hara, ed. "Awakening the Silent Majority: The Changing
Role of Women in my Church, Past Present and Future,"
Auburn Studies in Education, 1975.

[15]Laura Judd to Lydia Finney, 10 Dec. 1832; Charlotte
Baldwin to Mrs. Sophronial Baldwin, 7 October 1829, HMCS;
Thurston, Life and Times, 101; Sybil Bingham, Diary, 90-91.
The women's different experience of time (the men suffered
few interruptions) illustrates the dilemmas fostered by the
intersection of family time and historical time, concepts
that Hareven explores in Family Time and Industrial Time,
1-8.

[16]Sybil Bingham, Diary, 98; Thurston, Life and Times,
120. For a discussion of similar concerns, see Lois A. Boyd
and R. Douglas Brackenridge, Presbyterian Women in America:
Two Centuries of a Quest for Status, [Westport: Greenwood
Press, 1983] Chapter Ten; and Clifford Drury, ed., First
White Women over the Rockies, [Glendale: Arthur H. Clark,
1963], 127, 147 for the experiences of missionaries in
Oregon. The resolution that all these missionary women
reached, that of living vicariously through their husbands,
is a classic example of the accomodations that Hanna Papanek
describes in "Men, Women and Work: Reflections on the
Two-Person Career," 856-864.

[17]Thurston, Life and Times, 114; Sybil Bingham, Diary,
45b.

[18]Hiram Bingham, A Residence of Twenty One Years in the
Sandwich Islands [Hartford: H. Huntington, 1849], 331-333;
Miller, Fathers and Sons, Chapter Two.

[19]H. Bingham et. al. to Jeremiah Evarts, 20 March 1823,
HMCS; Daniel Tyerman and George Bennett to ABCFM in
Missionary Herald, April 1823, 104.

[20]H. Bingham to Jeremiah Evarts, 15 October 1828, HMCS.

[21]Thurston, Life and Times, 148; Bingham, A Residence,
333 disputes Thurston's figures, citing 19 children sent
away, 26 leaving with their parents and 3 orphaned children
who returned to the mainland, for a total of 48 children in
a twenty-seven year period compared to Thurston's 58 in 20

years. The two agree however, that this issue was one of the
most critical that the Mission faced.

[22]H. Bingham to Jeremiah Evarts, 15 October 1828, HMCS;
Samuel Whitney quoted in Thurston, Life and Times, 118;
Bingham, A Residence, 331-333.

[23]Sybil Bingham to Mrs. Willard, 30 November 1828, HMCS.

[24]Thurston, Life and Times, 101

[25]Ibid., 101-102.

[26]Ibid., 76, 84-85.

[27]Ibid., 135, 83; T. Walter Herbert, Marquesan
Encounters: Melville and the Meaning of Civilization,
[Cambridge: Harvard University Press, 1980], 24-30; for
discussions of similar reactions and efforts, see Hiram
Bingham, Jr., Voyage to Abaiang, Vol. II, HMCS passim, in
which he discusses the locale and structure of his mission
on the island of Abaiang and that of his colleagues elsewhere in Micronesia.

[28]Ibid., 98, 101.

[29]Ibid., 139. For a contemporary discussion of the
schools the missionary children attended, see Charles de
Varigney, Fourteen Years in the Sandwich Islands, 1855-1868
[Honolulu: University Press of Hawaii, 1981], 151-153,
189-192. The members of the mission reflected upon its
alteration after the pioneers departed and their memories
were especially revived when tales of new pioneer missions,
those in the Marquesans in the 1830s, and in Micronesia two
decades later, filtered back to Honolulu and the mainland.
Lucy Thurston commented, after receiving a letter from a
woman in the Marquesan Mission, that her "situation there is
quite unlike ours now at the Sandwich Islands. But it
reminds me of other years. Mrs. Armstrong writes that she
would as soon trust herself in the mouth of a lion, as out
of the house alone. We who have seen society in its heathen
state can better form an idea of the import of that
expression, and better realize the dangers with which she is
surrounded," [Life and Times, 117]. Another sympathethic
missionary was Hiram Bingham, Sr., whose son and daughter-
in-law established a new mission in the Gilbert Islands
(Kiribati) in the 1850s. In letters in which he consoled
them over the loss of their first child, and encouraged them
not to despair over the immense difficulties they faced, he
revealed an empathy and compassion that perhaps only another
pioneer missionary could have shown. See Hiram Bingham, Sr.
to Hiram Bingham, Jr and Clara Bingham, passim, Bingham
Family Papers, Yale University.

CHARLES W. FORMAN

PLAYING CATCH-UP BALL: THE HISTORY OF

FINANCIAL DEPENDENCE IN PACIFIC ISLAND CHURCHES

One of the problems of the so-called developing
nations, as they enter the world economic system, is that
they seem trapped in a position of dependence on the
developed nations. They hope to outgrow their
"under-development" and, through industrialization and
modernized agriculture, to reach a higher standard of living
and an independent economic position. But the projects
which they undertake for this purpose are too expensive for
them and require large loans or grants from abroad. The
loans which have been secured create mountains of debt which
threaten to swamp their economies. Furthermore, the
developed countries are always forging ahead with new
economic advances, so that the efforts at catching up are
constantly frustrated. The costs of industrialization mount
ever higher as technology becomes more sophisticated and as
the prices of machinery and energy rise with inflation. The
patterns of social service which are copied from the
developed areas become constantly more expensive. The
result seems to be that peoples who had an independent, if
simple, economic existence in the past become marginalized
and dependent in a world economic system where they are
always the poor. They are always looking for help from
their wealthier neighbors and adjusting their own plans and
projects to fit in with the interests and preferences of
prospective donors.

This common pattern of international economic life can
be seen even in the churches of the developing nations.
Many churches in Asia and Africa have struggled long with

the stubborn problem of economic dependence. Since their early days they have received funds from Western missionary agencies and habits of dependence, once established, have been hard to break. They, like their homelands, often find that they exist as the poor in a world economic system, that they are ever looking for help from wealthier churches and often adjusting their programs in accordance with the desires of prospective donors. They recognize that they need to stand on their own feet financially. They sense that if they are to be a continuing, indigenous part of Asian or African life they should not remain as economic dependencies of Europe or America. In fact any solid success in the planting of Christianity in Asia and Africa must be seen as contingent, to a considerable degree, on whether the Asian and African chuches can become self-supporting. This fact was recognized by the main missionary thinkers of the mid-nineteenth century and has been one of the principles of mission policy ever since. But the full implementation of that principle has, in the majority of cases, been long delayed and is still not completed.

The churches of the Pacific Islands have had a distinctive history in regard to this problem. For the most part they have not been as dependent as their African and Asian counterparts, but still the broad outlines of this common international pattern are visible among them. Just how serious the problem has been, how they have faced it and how successfully they have dealt with it, needs to be explored.[1]

Before the European explorers and the missionaries arrived upon the scene, religious life in the Pacific Islands was, of course, fully self-sufficient. Whatever its costs may have been, they were borne by the local people with no dependence on the outside world. In many areas there were priests or mediums who were supported by donations, usually of food, sometimes of bark cloth or other necessities, given them by the people. Such priests often opposed the introduction of Christianity because it threatened their livelihood and prestige. Where there were no priests there were still offerings made at the spirit shrines from the local food supply. At times the burden of these offerings could be heavy. Christian evangelists in Melanesia occasionally commended their new faith to the people because their god did not require the sacrifice of large numbers of pigs as did the traditional spirits.[2]

At the village level the people usually succeeded in making Christianity a self-supporting religion. The patterns of local self-support were established by the earliest missions. The London Missionary Society and the American Board of Commissioners for Foreign Missions, both of them predominantly Congregationalist bodies, along with the British-based Methodist Missionary Society, were the first missions in the Pacific in the modern period. These missions expected their village churches to be financially independent from the beginning. The same was true of two of the later missions, the Lutherans, who came to New Guinea at the end of the nineteenth century, and of the South Sea Evangelical Mission which came to Malaita in the Solomons at the beginnning of the twentieth. Through these various missions the pattern of local self-support was firmly established in the major churches of Tahiti, the Leeward and Austral Islands, Niue, Malaita, the Marshalls, the Carolines, and large sections of New Guinea Territory.

At first this was done with almost no use of cash. The people erected a house for their pastor, as they erected their own church building, and they gave land for the pastor's use on which he could grow food for himself. They also made offerings of food and other goods to the pastor

and in some islands such as Samoa and Tuvalu these were
sufficient to relieve him of the need to cultivate his own
land. In all these churches that have been mentioned the
whole cost of supporting the village pastor and the village
church was borne by the local people.

The other missions which came to the Pacific were not
so committed to local self-support. The Presbyterians, who
were the earliest and largest church in Vanuatu, began in a
self-supporting way but later used foreign funds to pay the
local teachers and evangelists.[3] The Anglicans who began
the first churches in the Solomon Islands and on the east
coast of Papua, were accustomed from the beginning to paying
the local priests from their mission funds. Even the London
Missionary Society, when it came to Papua in the late
nineteenth century, adopted the practice of paying the local
pastors with foreign funds. This was because its first
pastors were Polynesians whom it had brought in, not local
men whom the local people might be expected to support.
Most important, the Roman Catholic missions, which became
the the largest and most widespread missions in the Pacific,
expected no contributions from the village people. The
Catholic catechists, who were the men in charge of the local
congregations, were given what few supplies they needed by
the missionaries. In all these missions--Presbyterian,
Anglican and Catholic--the local pastor, catechist or priest
was expected to grow much of his own food and the local
people often provided the labor, if not the materials, to
erect the church building, so the amount of dependence on
the mission was not large. The crucial thing, however, was
that the people did not feel that the continuing support of
the church was their responsibility.[4]

Local schools were financed in the same way as local
churches, which was to be expected since school and church
were practically one at the beginning, the pastor or

catechist serving as schoolteacher and the church building serving as schoolhouse. In those denominations where the village church was self-supporting, the school was too, and where the village church was not, the school was not.[5]

Taking the Pacific churches as a whole, it is evident that in the majority of cases when Christianity came to the islands it was able to operate at the village level in the same way that the indigenous religion had operated. If it required larger financial contributions than had the indigenous beliefs, they were not overwhelmingly larger and the villages were easily able to provide them. There was no great effort required to catch up with expensive new patterns of operation.

But Christianity did introduce costly new patterns of operation on the national level, if the word "national" can be used to include those territories which as yet had no consciousness of being nations. There were higher levels of education, namely secondary schools and theological seminaries, which could not be provided in each village but which had to be developed in central locations for a whole country. And there were the costs for the central operations of church life, central administration, mission boats or ships, travel costs for supervisors of village churches, and the salaries of foreign missionaries. These costs introduced a whole new level of religious expenditure which the islands had not known before and which they would have to carry if they were to provide for their own religious needs. Here was something to catch up with.

For the central schools and seminaries the churches quickly developed a pattern of operation which fit well into the simple economy of the islands. They had to depend, it is true, on foreign missionary teachers, and this was an important point of dependence on an outside resource. The

students, however, were largely self-supporting. Studies
were usually limited to half of each day. The other half
was spent by the students in growing their own vegatables,
catching their own fish, or working on the construction or
upkeep of the school buildings and grounds.[6] Under this
regimen academic standards could not rise very high, but
economic standards were appropriate to local conditions.
Occasionally the students erected impressive school
buildings. The imposing Gothic edifice of the Methodist
seminary in Samoa was constructed entirely by students
between 1912 and 1919, under the guidance of a missionary,
though this meant that several classes of future pastors
learned extremely little about their church or faith and
much about stone and plaster.[7]

There remained the costs of the central operations of
the church. If these could be paid for and the missionary
teachers be supported, the island churches could be regarded
as financially independent. To reach that higher level of
self-sufficiency required a greater effort.

The first and most popular way to raise funds for the
central operations was to hold a mission festival every year
at which people would make large contributions. There was
great rivalry associated with these occasions. Sometimes it
was rivalry between families in the same village, sometimes
it was rivalry between villages. Announcements were always
made of the amount that each family gave, or that other
villages were contributing, and each tried to outdo the
others. These mission festivals were held in practically all
Methodist, Congregational, and Presbyterian areas, but were
not common among the Catholics, Lutherans or Anglicans. It
was partly because of this difference that the latter three
denominations consistently lagged behind in the support of
the church above the village level.

The funds which were collected in the mission festival were normally sent off to London or Paris or Sydney as a contribution to the work of the mission societies which had created the island churches. Thus they were not directly used for the operation of those churches at the national level. But in fact the mission societies were paying costs of the national operation of the churches and those costs came to more than the contributions from the islands, except in a few cases to be considered shortly. So in actuality the funds sent abroad were part of the costs of national operation. Not a few Europeans in the Pacific islands, including some government officials, complained about this drain on the island economies and wrote reports to their home governments or articles in the press attacking the practice of sending funds abroad. Sometimes, when it was shown to them that more was coming into the islands than was being taken out, they withdrew their complaints. More often the complaints continued. And there were a few island countries which for a time did send out more than came in. In these countries the complaints were justified. Yet at the same time the achievement of those countries needs to be recognized. The churches of those lands proved that they could put an end to all economic dependence.[8]

The first country in which a church achieved full self-support was Tonga. There, in 1862, the king drew up, with the help of a Methodist missionary, Shirley Baker, legislation which put an end to feudal exactions. Once free of such exactions, the common people began raising cash crops and their contributions to the mission festivals increased greatly. By 1866 they were giving more than enough to cover all church expenses including the salaries of the foreign missionaries.

Three years later Shirley Baker became chairman of the mission and succeeded in raising contributions still higher

by taking unprecedented and extreme measures to incite
competition. He divided congregations into teams and put in
charge of each some notable person whose prestige in society
would be involved in the achievement of his team. On the
day of the collection young men on horseback would ride
around, carrying the colors of their team and urging their
cohorts to larger contributions. Credit was made available
for those who wished to give more than their present means
allowed. The inflated amounts thus raised were sent to
Sydney, according to the usual practice. The mission was
clearly draining money out of the country and this caused
dissatisfaction among many Tongans, including the king.
Later, when Baker became prime minister, he turned against
the mission and was able to use that particular
dissatisfaction, along with others, to persuade the king to
lead in the formation of a new church independent of
Australia. Both the new national church thus begun and the
smaller mission-related church which survived, continued to
be fully self-supporting.[9]

The next major churches to reach national self-support
were in Samoa.[10] The Samoan economy was flourishing during
World War I and in that period the two Protestant churches,
Congregational and Methodist, voted to take on all their
national costs including the costs of foreign missionaries.
In both cases the mission societies which had founded the
churches suggested this action and the Methodists were also
inspired by the example of Tonga.[11]

These achievements by Tonga and Samoa were unique in
the world. They represented the fulfillment of the goal
which Protestant missions generally had set before
themselves since the middle of the nineteenth century,
namely that they should create national churches which would
be self-supporting, as well as being self-governing and
self-propagating. None of the churches of Africa and Asia

had reached that goal, if the costs of foreign missionaries were included as part of what was meant by being self-supporting. The small lands of the Pacific were now held up as a model for the churches of the East.[12]

But the model was not to be copied. Even in the Pacific, other lands did not go as far as Tonga and Samoa. Fiji, which had the largest of the older churches, might have been expected to follow the same course and the Australian Methodist Mission board had hopes that it would. But Fijian contributions never covered the cost of foreign missionaries and when, in the 1920s, it was agreed that Fiji would at least handle all its other costs, the lean years of the Great Depression ensued and undermined the agreement. The Fijian church had to go heavily into debt to Australia in order to cover even its internal expenses. Not till 1943, when masses of foreign troops brought new wealth into the country, could the loans be paid back and Fiji at last stand on its own feet.[13]

The economic depression of the 1930s also forced Tonga and Samoa to fall back from their full support of foreign workers. The price of copra, the source of cash for the people, plummetted and it became almost impossible to keep up the old level of contributions. The mission sending agencies in Sydney and London recognized the islanders' plight and both offered to reduce the churches' responsibilities. The offers were accepted with great relief. From then on the islands paid only part of the cost of foreign missionaries and at times none of it, though they continued to pay all other national church costs.[14]

The world's only experiments in full local support for foreign missionaries had not been a success. The experiments expected more than the island churches could easily provide and they inevitably became a heavy burden when economic conditions were adverse. At all times they fomented a certain amount of envy and resentment because the

locally paid Westerners required so much more money to live
on than did the indigenous workers. The new arrangements
stirred additional tensions whenever the local paymasters
wanted to make clear their new power in relation to their
former leaders, as when it was proposed, though not voted,
in the Samoan Congregational Church's General Assembly that
the pay of missionaries be handed out by the local pastors
publicly and in cash.[15]

If full support for foreign workers proved too
difficult or too problematic, support of the total internal
national costs of the church seemed to be increasingly
possible and achievable. Fiji, as has been noted, achieved
that level of support by 1943. Many other churches reached
that point during the middle decades of the twentieth
century. The main Protestant churches of Kiribati and
Tuvalu, of New Caledonia and the Loyalties, of Nauru and
Niue, of the Marshalls and the eastern Carolines, of the
Cook Islands and of parts of the Solomons were in this
category.[16]

Tahiti and the other Society Islands did more than
cover their internal costs. Like Tonga and Samoa they made
significant contributions to the support of foreign
missionaries, though unlike those other lands they never
undertook to provide the complete support. In fact for a
time at the beginning of this century Tahiti had to beg from
the Paris Mission for the support of its own pastors,
because the French government in a fit of anti-clericalism
suddenly cut off the money which it had long provided for
them. Gradually the loss was made good from local
contributions and no more begging was necessary. [17]

It is evident through all this that the churches which
achieved financial autonomy at the national level were the
same churches which had originally started out with it at
the village level. Mission policy and expectations at the

start were apparently of crucial importance in giving church
members a sense of responsibility and encouraging them to
enlarge that responsibility. Initial policy was not
completely determinative, however. At least one church
which had begun with self-support at the village level,
could not reach it at the national level. This was the
Lutheran Church in New Guinea Territory. The failure was
largely due to the fact that the national operation became
so expensive. American Lutherans came in after World War I
to help and to supplement the old German work, and with
these combined forces and much American money, this became
the largest Protestant mission in the world and doubtless
one of the most expensive. By the 1960s the budget was over
a million dollars a year.[18]   To balance this Lutheran
story, however, there were some churches which had not been
self-supporting at the village level in the early days,
which became so and then went on by mid-century to become
self-supporting at the national level. The prime example of
this was the Methodist church in the New Britain area. The
Methodists of New Britain were located chiefly in the highly
developed and productive area around Raboul, so they
enjoyed an economic strength which allowed them to take
responsibility for all their central as well as village
costs by 1938. By the 1960s they were also helping with the
missionary costs.[19] The Methodists in the Solomons moved
more slowly, but by 1963 they were supporting all their
indigenous workers, except for medical officers. By about
that time, too, the Papua Eklesia, the church developed by
the London Missionary Society which had originally been so
dependent at the village level, was supporting its own
village pastors and was well on the way toward taking care
of its own expenses.[20]

     Except for the Anglicans, Lutherans and Catholics,
then, the battle for self-support at the national level had

been essentially won in most of the churches of the Pacific by the middle decades of the twentieth century.[21]

    But with one battle won, another loomed. Self-support covered only the costs that the churches had already known. In the islands of the western Pacific the years around the middle of the century saw the appearance of large new costs. The governments of those islands, namely Vanuatu, Kiribati, Tuvalu, New Caledonia, the Solomons, and Papua New Guinea, became involved in a great drive to improve educational and medical services, and called on the churches for help.

    In the more easterly islands the governments had built up these services in earlier years and required little new help from the churches. But in the western islands little had been done except for the very simple village schools taught by pastors. Now the governments gathered the church leaders together in conferences and urged them to throw new resources into the advancement of education and medicine. They promised new initiatives of their own and they also promised to provide funds for the churches if they would do their share.

    Here opened up a prospect for increased usefulness of the churches, but also for a great increase in their financial liabilities. A new dependency threatened to take the place of the old one which had been so widely overcome. There was considerable debate in the churches, but everywhere they finally decided to accept the governments' challenge.

    In each of the western territories the primary schools were brought up to new standards established by government. Real secondary schools were begun by the churches for the first time. Teachers' colleges were established where none had existed before. All this called for many more foreign missionaries as teachers and much more foreign money to pay

the bills.   In the Solomon Islands the churches were soon
using half their missionaries and half their budgets for
education.   The promised government funds helped, but they
covered less than half the increased costs.   In Papua New
Guinea the churches' educational cost went up form $222,000
to $907,000 in eleven years, 1953-1964, while the
government's grants went up from $81,000 to $489,000.
Clearly the churches were being saddled with an enormous new
financial burden, which could be paid for only by new funds
from abroad.

Eventually the new program broke down, in part because
of inadequate funding.[22]   Even with the increased aid from
abroad, the churches could not pay their teachers the
salaries which the governments were able to offer in their
own schools.   Educating a pupil in Papua New Guinea church
schools cost only one-sixth of what it cost in government
schools.   Sometimes the churches were able to hire more
dedicated teachers who were willing to work for less, but
more often they just had to hire less capable and less well
trained teachers.   Both the government and the churches were
dissatisfied with this situation.   Eventually some churches
announced that they were going to turn their primary schools
over to the government.   The Kiribati Protestants and the
Vanuatu Presbyterians announced this in 1965, and all the
major bodies in the Solomons did so in 1974 or soon after.
In Papua New Guinea the government took the initiative and
convinced the churches that they should turn over their
schools to a national system in 1970.[23]

Medical service presented a picture similar to
education.   In Vanuatu, the Solomons and Papua New Guinea,
the churches increased their medical services enormously
starting in the 1950s.   The governments expanded their
service at the same time and helped the churches.   But
government aid did not meet the increased costs.   In Papua

New Guinea in 1964, the churches were providing half the nation's medical care and were spending twice as much as they received in government grants. In the Solomons the disproportion between expenditures and grants was even greater. Medical service was a tremendously expensive matter and far beyond what the churches could ever hope to undertake unaided from abroad. Lutherans in New Guinea found medical work using up one-third of their mission funds. The ruling body of the Presbyterian Church in Vanuatu declared that medical work was one field they should never try to "take over in any way from the overseas churches."[24]

The retreat from medicine was not as complete as from education, but there was the same kind of movement. The Papua New Guinea government in 1974 agreed to pay the full salaries of all the medical workers in the churches and the Vanuatu government took over the main Presbyterian hospital. Some church-financed medical service continued, however.

In all the western islands the huge increase in costs and consequent increased level of dependency which had been undertaken at the beginning of the 1950s were largely finished by the end of the 1970s. The churches had, in a way, overcome another dependency, this time by withdrawing from most of the costs.

But recently one more hurdle has been thrown up, much smaller than the previous ones, yet illustrating the continuity of the problem. Just as the costs of economic development constantly increase, so the costs of being a modern church are always rising. The Pacific islands are now part of an interrelated world, the "global village." The churches, therefore, cannot live each in its own group of islands. They have to reach out to the whole Pacific and the whole world. An outreaching movement of ecumenical

contacts has transformed church life. But it has also added
a new level of expense and created a new area of dependence.
Within the island nations new councils of churches have
sprung up. Some of these are informal operations with no
significant expenses, but others, such as those in Fiji, the
Solomons and Papua New Guinea, are larger and, at least
initially, have had to depend on foreign money for their
costs.[25]   Outside   the   national   borders,   trans-Pacific
organizations have been forged, such as the South Pacific
Anglican   Council   and   the   two   Roman   Catholic   bishops'
conferences. These have involved heavy travel expenses and
have required more subsidies, either directly or indirectly,
from outside the region. Most noticeable of all is the
Pacific Conference of Churches, the major ecumenical body
binding together the churches of the islands. By 1981 it
received over 95% of its budget from outside sources. In
1982, in a desperate effort to become less dependent, it
dropped most of its programs and most of its staff. Thereby
the problem of dependence was decreased but it was not fully
overcome.

Another cost of being a modern church able to speak to
the modern world is a more expensive kind of ministerial
training. The old theological schools, where the students
supported themselves by their daily labor, could not produce
ministers able to answer the questions of modern young
people educated in schools where they devoted their full
time to study. The level of theological education had to be
raised and the ministerial students had to be supported at
church expense so that they also could give their full time
to their studies. New international institutions of higher
theological training were required, such as the Pacific
Theological College founded by Protestants and the Pacific
Regional Seminary founded by Catholics. These new
institutions remained largely dependent on foreign funding.

The improvements in theological education were parallelled by similar costly improvements in church administration. New specialization in church leadership was needed to deal with a more complex society. Thus, the old and traditional Evangelical Church of Tahiti showed during its first decade of independence a large increase in its administrative personnel and a corresponding six-fold increase in its budget. The impecunious Kiribati Protestant Church found the number of executives at its headquarters increased from three to seventeen between 1967 and 1983. The church reported: "operating costs have gone up sharply in the last few years."[26]

At the same time new calls for service were heard by the churches. The freshly independent island nations were launching new economic development projects and were struggling with increasing urbanization. The churches, which had been released from many of the expenses of educational and medical service, here saw new opportunities before them. They desired to help with national improvements, such as better agriculture, the provision of water supplies, the humanizing of life for newcomers in the cities, and the enriching of life in the villages. These new efforts were usually undertaken through specific projects for which grants were requested from churches and church councils in other parts of the world.

The result of these new developments was that the churches were now required to catch up with a range of expenses which they had never known before. The financial independence which they had achieved in earlier times, did not cover all the new costs. In some churches the amount of dependence was only marginal, but in others it was serious. In Papua New Guinea a Lutheran writer said that the churches of that country were shockingly dependent and that dependence on foreign money was growing. Even the most independent of the major churches of that country, the

United Church, was judged in 1976 to be still far too dependent.[27] The traditionally self-reliant Kiribati Protestant Church increased its levies on its own members but also had to ask for increased donations from abroad, while the traditionally dependent Catholics in Micronesia reported that, though they made constant efforts to increase contributions, the increase could not overtake the steadily rising expenses.[29] Modernizing evidently had negative as well as positive consequences.

It has apparently been a long game of "catch-up ball" which the island churches have been playing, a game in which they have been behind and have constantly been at a disadvantage. Most of them have made great efforts at being self-supporting and have all but achieved that goal, but then new expenses have appeared and have pushed the goal further away from them.

In most of the larger churches, the amount of continuing dependence does not appear to be of serious proportions. In the Methodist churches and those with a connection to the former London Missionary Society or The French Reformed Church, any continuing dependence at the present time is only for the maintenance of certain programs of social services, church advancement and inter-church cooperation which are not essential to the life of the church. The dependence on outside finances therefore is marginal and could be ended if these programs were dropped.

In other churches, however, it must be acknowledged that the amount of dependence is still very serious. The donations of their own members have never come close to catching up with their expenses. Not only their programs of cooperation and service, but also their whole operations

require large amounts of funding from other sources than
their own members. They could hardly survive in their
present form if the funds were cut off. The bodies in this
category are the Lutherans and Anglicans in Papua New
Guinea, the Anglicans in the Solomons and the Roman
Catholics throughout the islands. Two smaller, but
widespread bodies, which also belong in this catergory,
though they have not been mentioned thus far, are the
Mormons and the Seventh-Day Adventists.[30]

Clearly it is mission policy, as suggested earlier,
that has been the major factor in creating independence or
allowing continued dependence. The lines of separation
between the two types of churches do not follow territorial
divisions, though this might be expected since some
territories have much less wealth than others. The dry
atolls of Tuvalu provide far less wealth than the mines and
plantations of Papua New Guinea, yet the Tuvalu Church is
largely self-supporting while most of the major churches of
Papua New Guinea are heavily dependent. Nor do the lines of
separation fall in accordance with the age of the churches,
which, if it were the case, would suggest that older
churches had a better chance of growing into self-support.
The Anglican Church in the Solomon Islands is half a century
older than the South Sea Evangelical Church, yet the one
derives most of its income from the investments of its
supporting mission in New Zealand[31] while the other derives
practically its whole income from its own members. The
lines of separation do, however, follow denominational lines
very closely. All the Methodist, Congregational and
Reformed churches, whether they are in rich territories or
poor, whether they are older or younger, are essentially
self-supporting. All the Catholic, Anglican, Lutheran,
Mormon and Adventist churches, whatever their age and
wherever they may be depend on essential subsidies from

abroad. This denominational division indicates that the differences between the churches stem from the policies of their founding missions. Those missions which from an early stage worked for self-support founded churches that could stand on their own feet. Those missions which allowed churches to be dependent for many years eventually found such dependence to be almost unbreakable. It is hard to persuade people to pay for something they are accustomed to receiving free.

Yet though there are major differences among the churches, it is evident that all of them retain at least some degree of dependence and that, in the case of the more self-sustaining types, this is the result of new levels of expense which continue to arise and with which they have not yet caught up. All of them, therefore, are to some extent afflicted by a psychology of dependence, having to adjust their plans and programs to the interests and priorities of outsiders.

It is true that most of the Pacific churches have come a longer way toward financial independence than have the churches of tropical Africa or southern Asia. It is also true that in comparison to some other institutions in the developing nations many of them have shown a commendable self-reliance. But dependence has not been ended. The game is not yet won.

NOTES

[1]For those unfamiliar with the ecclesiastical geography
of the Pacific Islands, the following information will be
helpful, since it is assumed in this article.
    Tahiti and the other Society Islands have as their
oldest and largest church the Evangelical Church begun by
the London Missionary Society (LMS) and subsequently
assisted by the French Protestants.
    The Marqueses are heavily Roman Catholic in affi-
liation.
    The Cook Islanders are mostly adherents of the
Protestant Church begun by the LMS.
    Samoa's largest church is the Congregational Church
begun by the LMS, but Catholics and Methodists form significant minorities.
    In Tuvalu the only church until recently has been the
LMS Congregational body. In Kiribati this church and the
Catholics fairly evenly divide the population.
    Fijians are nearly all Methodists, but the Indians of
Fiji constitute the one large group of South Pacific people
who are outside any Christian Church.
    Tonga is mostly Methodist, though divided into several
branches of that church.
    Vanuatu's principal church has always been the
Presbyterian, though in certain islands the Anglicans and
the Church of Christ are predominant and the Catholics are
widespread and influential.
    New Caledonia and the Loyalty Islands have long had the
Catholic and the Evangelical (French Reformed) churches as
their principal bodies, the Catholics predominating in New
Caledonia and the Evangelicals in the Loyalties.
    The Solomon Islands have a cut-up religious geography.
The Anglicans are the oldest continuing church and they
dominate Ysabel and some other islands. The Catholics are
strong in Guadalcanal and elsewhere. The South Sea
Evangelical Church is strong in Malaita. The Methodists are
the main church in the Western Solomons and the Seventh Day
Adventists are also significant there.
    In the Bismarck Archipelago and Bougainville the
Catholics and the Methodists have been the principal church
groups from the beginning.
    In Papua most of the south coast has been the preserve
of the LMS, the east coast of the Anglicans, and the eastern
off-shore islands of the Methodists.
    The former mandated territory of New Guinea saw the
Lutherans and the Catholics as the first churches and they

have continued to be the largest. But the recently opened
Highland areas are filled with a variety of newly introduced
churches.
    In Micronesia the Congregationalists, begun by missions
from America, have been the traditional church, though
Catholics and some newer Protestant groups have also become
strong.
    The Catholics are also important as a minority group in
any of the above areas where they have not been mentioned.
Mormons have become an important minority in the Polynesian
areas.
    Hawaii and New Zealand are not included in this study
because the original island peoples form only a small frac-
tion of the church members of those lands.

    [2]David Hilliard, "Protestant Missions in the Solomon
Islands 1849-1942," Ph.D. thesis, Australian National
University, 1966, 478. Darrell Whiteman, Melanesians and
Missionaries, [Pasadena: William Carey Library, 1983], 245.

    [3]J. Graham Miller, Live. A History of Church Planting
in the New Hebrides to 1880, Book one. [Sydney: Christian
Education Committee, General Assembly of Australia, 1978],
151-154. They did not return to local self-support till
well into the twentieth century. Presbyterian Church of
Australia, General Assembly Minutes 1964, 171. B. Nottage,
New Hebrides Calling, [Auckland: Presbyterian Church of New
Zealand, 1940], 17.

    [4]For the Catholics the missionaries not only brought in
funds from abroad but also developed industries and plantations as a source of financial support. The greatest area
for this was German New Guinea where the government
encouraged European acquisition of land. The Lutherans,
too, and even the Methodists, secured land in that territory. But the Catholics were the chief ones to work in this
way. A report in 1935, after Australia had taken over
control from Germany, showed the Methodists with five
thousand acres, the Lutherans with twelve thousand and the
Catholics with nearly 110,000 (Harold Davis, "Auctioneers of
Paradise." American Mercury 36 (1935), 219). Clearly the
support of the chuch through plantations was primarily a
Catholic phenomenon. It could well be claimed that since
the plantations and industries were located within the
Pacific territories, they represented a form of indigenous,
rather than foreign support. Yet they did not represent
self-support within the village scene and they did not allow
for the development of a sense of responsibility for the
church on the part of the villages. Plantations were a primary source of Catholic funding only in New Guinea Territory
and New Caledonia. In other lands Catholics continued to
depend primarily on contributions from abroad.

[5]School books, of which the Bible was the chief, were
the first items for which international exchange, and therefore money, was needed. Books were usually purchased with
local funds. When the Bible was first printed in the
Tahitian language, the people paid for it in coconut oil,
which could be exported and turned into cash. See Jack
Beeching, An Open Path: Christian Missionaries 1515-1914,
[London: Hutchinson, 1979], 96. In Vanuatu, Bibles and
other school books were paid for by exporting arrowroot,
which the mission taught the people to make from a local
plant and which was often marketed by women's church groups
in New Zealand. J. Graham Miller, Live. A History of
Church Planting in the New Hebrides to 1880, Book One,
151-154. Willian Gunn, The Gospel in Futuna with Chapters
on the Islands of the New Hebrides, the People, their
Customs, Religious Beliefs, etc, [London: Hodder &
Stoughton, 1914], 145.

[6]Sometimes the home congregations or families of the
students helped by sending non-perishable food like dried
fish or coconut molasses. Often the students built their
own houses. In New Britain until very recently married students would come to school six months ahead of their families and build a thatch house and plant a garden which would
be ready to feed the wife and children when they arrived.

[7]The South Sea Evangelical Mission was strict about its
rule of self-support not only in regard to village churches
and schools but also in regard to the central boarding
schools. When these were begun in the 1930s they were
built, operated and supported entirely by the Malaitans.
David Hilliard, "The South Sea Evangelical Mission in The
Solomon Islands: The Foundation Years?" Journal of Pacific
History 4 (1969), 60.

[8]Examples of the complaints by Europeans are found in
Richard Deeken, "Schulinspekto auf Reisen," in Manuia
Samoa. Samoanische Reiseskizzen und Beobachtungen, [Berlin
and Oldenburg: Gerhard Stalling, 1901], 111; Henri Lebeau,
"Le Christianisme et la musique populaire," in Otaheiti, au
pays de l'éternel été; [Paris: Librairie Armand Colin,
1911], 228-29; A. J. Viner, G. J. Williams, & Frank Lenwood,
Report of...Deputation to the South Seas and Papua (with
a chapter on the organization in Australia) June 1915-June
1916, [London: London Missionary Society, 1916], 122-23;
Norman Goodall, A History of the London Missionary Society
1895-1945, [London: Oxford University Press, 1954], 374;
Noel Rutherford, "Shirley Baker and the Kingdom of Tonga,"
Ph.D. thesis, Australian National University, 1966, 81-82.
Only in Viner (1916) is there reference, by mission repre-
sentatives,to a government official withdrawing his

complaints, and this claim of withdrawal seems contradicted
by government dispatches of three years later. Cf. C. H.
Rodwell, High Commissioner for the Western Pacific, to the
Secretary of State for the Colonies, Jan. 6, 1919, Public
Record Office, London. The London Missionary Society's
reply to this later complaint has been lost through war
damage, but the local missionary's reply is found in letters
of Sarah Jolliffe to Frank Lenwood, Nov. 29, 1919, and Dec.
21, 1919, Council for World Mission Archives, London.

[9]Noel Rutherford, "Shirley Baker and the Kingdom of
Tonga," 59-60, 76-83.

[10]There were some small islands which came to full self-
support before Samoa. The only islands of Lifou and Ouvea
in the Loyalties, where there was only one missionary, were
by 1915 contributing enough to the London Missionary Society
to pay the missionary's salary and all other expenses. A.
J. Viner et al. Report of...Deputation to the South Seas
and Papua (with a chapter on the organization in Australia)
June 1915-June 1916, 6.

[11]The Methodists also had a strong loyalty and a consequent readiness to make large contributions because of the
fact that they were a minority group. It was noticed that
Methodists in Samoa gave four times as much per capita to
the church as did Methodists in Fiji where they comprised
nearly the whole Fijian population. The suggestion for
self-support from the Methodist mission board in Australia
came about 1911 and was related to the fact that funds were
needed for new church development in the Western Pacific.
The Samoan Methodist approval of the suggestion came in
1914. See A. W. Thornley, "Fijian Methodism, 1874-1945.
The Emergence of a National Church," Ph.D. thesis,
Australian National University, 1979, 270-271. A. Harold
Wood, Overseas Missions of the Australian Methodist Church,
Melbourne Aldersgate Press, 1975, 320. The suggestion from
the Congregational mission, the London Missionary Society,
came in 1915, after contributions had already almost reached
the level of full self-support. A. J. Viner et al., Report
of...Deputation to the South Seas and Papua (with a chapter
on the organization in Australia) June 1915-1916, 85, 111.

[12]A. J. Viner, et al., Report of...Deputation to the
South Seas and Papua (with a chapter on the organisation in
Australia) June 1915-1916, 88.

[13]Fijian steps toward national self-support began in 1902
when the Australian mission board arranged that half the
collections taken up at the annual mission festivals would
be kept in the country for the central operations of the

church. Previously the whole amount had been sent to
Sydney. The other half, which continued to go to Sydney,
covered about one-third of the salaries of the missionaries
whom Australia sent to Fiji. See Methodist Church of
Australasia, Report and Recommendations of the Commission
appointed by the Mission Board to Visit the Fiji District,
1917, also Resolution of the Mission Board, [Sydney: Epworth
Printing and Publishing House], 1917, 40. Then, in 1911, a
new constitution was drawn up for the Fijian church which
planned for payment of all expenses including the missionaries' salaries. But in the next years there were severe
hurricanes and then, during World War I, the government
asked the people to contribute to its war chest. The result
was that the long-planned self-support did not materialize.
After the war it seemed that all the Fijian church could
hope for was to cover its internal expenses apart from the
cost of foreign missionaries. In 1923 it was agreed that
the whole amount of the mission festival collections would
be retained in the country for this purpose and in 1929 each
region of the church, known as a circuit, was also made
self-supporting. The depression destroyed the immediate
effectiveness of these plans, but in the long run the Fijian
Methodists were able to implement them. A. W. Thornley,
"Fijian Methodism, 1874-1945. The Emergence of a National
Church," Ph.D. thesis, Australian National University, 1979,
273, 324.

14The Methodists in Sydney offered to take on the whole
cost of the missionaries they sent to Tonga and Samoa and
this offer was accepted by those churches in 1934. Later
when the islands' circumstances improved, they began again
to contribute a portion of the missionary salaries. By 1948
Samoan Methodism was providing full support for its missionaries, but that support was dropped again in 1964 when the
missionaries saw that it was a burden to the church. See A.
Harold Wood, Overseas Missions of the Methodist Church, Vol.
I, Tonga and Samoa, 229, 324. South Pacific Missionary
Conference 1948, Report of Commission 3, in archives of
Australian Council of Churches, Sydney. Interview with
Piula College staff, April 1967. Tonga continued to pay a
large part of its missionaries' support. The London
Missionary Society at the time of the depression did not go
so far as to offer to take over all missionary support, but
it did offer to reduce the payments expected from the Samoan
Congregationalists. The Samoans then decided that they
would send 2000 annually rather than the 5000 which they
had been sending. This lower figure was enough to cover
about two-thirds of the missionary costs. Because between
1922 and 1927 the number of missionaries sent to the church
had been reduced from fourteen to ten, the original amount
was no longer needed. Even the reduced amount began to seem

galling to many Samoans because it smacked of a foreign
demand placed upon them, so it was later changed--in 1961--
to an unfixed amount of free will offerings. Norman
Goodall, A History of the London Missionary Society 1895-
1945, 374-785. Samoa District Committee V. A. Barradale,
Report of Rev. V. A. Barradale after Secretarial Visit to
the South Seas, Papua, Australia and New Zealand August
1926-June 1927 (with the Rev. G. J. Williams in Papua),
[London: London Missionary Society, 1927], 26-27, 29.
Norman Goodall, Report...after a Secretarial Visit to the
Pacific, [London: London Missionary Society], 1940, 33.
Stuart C. Craig, "Notes on a Secretarial Visit to Fiji, 16
April-17 May, 1961," Mimeographed, [London: London
Missionary Society], 1961, 5.

[15]Norman Goodall, A History of the London Missionary
Society 1895-1945, 374. Cf. Methodist Church of
Australasia, Report and recommendations of the Commission
appointed by the Mission Board to Visit the Fiji District,
1917, also the Resolution of the Mission Board, 7.

[16]The Cook Islands had a prosperous economy and were
essentially self-supporting already in the nineteenth century, but they continued to depend on the LMS for the salary
of their one or two missionaries and the services of the
mission ship. In the first part of the twentieth century,
London often urged them to follow in the path of Samoa, but
the Church did not have sufficient vitality in those days to
do so. It was not till the last missionary was withdrawn in
the 1960s and the mission ship was withdrawn in the 1970s
that all shreds of dependency ended. For the urging from
London cf. A. J. Viner et al., Report of...Deputation to the
South Seas and Papua (with a chapter on the organization in
Australia) June 1915-June 1916, 22, 32, 36-37; and in the
Council for World Mission Archives, F. Lenwood to H. Bond
James, Dec. 25, 1920; Dec. 24., 1924; Sept. 22, 1927.
Kiribati and Tuvalu followed essentially the same course as
the Cook Islands. The Evangelical Church of New Caledonia
and the Loyalty Islands was handling all its central expen-
ses by 1952 and in the 1960s this included not only its own
central educational institutions, but also assistance to the
Presbyterian high school in Vanuatu. Paris helped with some
of the travel costs of delegates to the General Synod. (E.
Schloesing, "Rapport de M. E. Schloesing sur son Voyage en
Océanie (Nov. 1951-Mar. 1952)". Mimeographed, Société de
Missions Evangéliques de Paris, 1952, 14; interviews with
treasurers of the church and of the Paris Mission, 1967).
The Presbyterians in Vanuatu made great efforts at increasing self-support and achieved it at the local level, but it
was reported at the Pacific Conference of Churches Assembly
in 1981, that they were still receiving very large sums from

Australia and New Zealand for their national operation. For
the changing situation in Micronesia see Charles W. Forman,
The Island Churches of the South Pacific: Emergence in the
Twentieth Century, [Maryknoll, N.Y.: Orbis Books, 1982],
63-64, 125. The South Sea Evangelical Mission in the
Solomons adhered strictly to its policy of self-support when
it helped the indigenous people form the South Sea
Evangelical Church in 1964.

[17]Minutes of the meeting of the Missionaries of the Paris
Society in the French Establishments in Oceania, Dec. 13-20,
1900. L. de Pomaret to the Committee of the Society of
Missions of Paris, June 4, 1901. Both in Paris Evangelical
Mission Archives. The recovery is shown by the statement in
Edward Ahnne, Dans les Iles du Pacifique, [Paris: Société
des Missions Evangéliques, 1931], 42-44, which states that
the 1927 contributions nearly covered the cost of the
Mission. E. Schloesing, "Rapport de M. E. Schloesing sur
son Voyage en Océanie (Nov. 1951-Mar 1952)," 29, says that
contributions from French Polynesia, covered two-thirds of
the Mission's costs in those islands. A. Roux of the Paris
headquarters stated in an interview in 1966 that because
costs had increased, the 1960-62 contributions equaled only
one-ninth or one-eighth of the Mission's costs. After 1966,
contributions soared along with costs because of the new
money in the islands from tourism and atomic bomb tests.

[18]Albert and Sylvia Fredrichs, Anutu Conquers in New
Guinea: The Story of 70 Years of Mission Work in New
Guinea, revised edition, [Minneapolis: Augsburg Press,
1969], 145-146.

[19]R. G. Williams, The United Church in Papua, New Guinea
and the Solomon Islands, [Rabaul: Trinity Press., 1972],
145. Neville Threlfall, One Hundred Years in the Islands.
The Methodist/United Church in the New Guinea Islands
Region 1875-1975, [Rabaul: United Church, 1975], 208. In
the earlier years, 1927 and 1936, the Methodists had temporarily covered all central expenses. Methodist Church New
Britain, District Chairman's Report, 1936. Methodist
Mission Archives, Sydney.

[20]The Methodists and the Papua Ekalesia joined together
in 1968, along with an independent congregation in Port
Moresby, to form the United Church of Papua New Guinea and
the Solomon Islands. This body has had the least dependence
on foreign funding of all the major churches of Papua New
Guinea. Brian Turner, "A Nation of Beggars?" Catalyst 6,
no. 2, 98-99.

[21]The Presbyterians also offer something of an exception
as indicated in note 16 above.

22Charles W. Forman, The Island Churches of the South Pacific. Emergence in the Twentieth Century, 182-192.

23In New Caledonia alone were the churches allowed to keep their schools and also provided with sufficient government subsidies to cover all their expenses, including salaries at the same level as those in government schools. One western area does not fit the general picture. That is the American-ruled area of Micronesia. There the churches took on greatly increased educational expenses, improving their elementary schools and starting their first high schools, without any promise of government aid. American tradition did not favor state support for church schools, and so the government gave encouragement but not funds. Eventually the government's own educational system improved so much that the oldest Protestant church, the Congregationalists, closed their high school on Ponape in 1973, and some of the smaller Catholic schools were not rebuilt when damaged by hurricanes. But the Catholics, in general, hung onto their fine educational system even though their dependency on Catholics in America was high.

24Presbyterian Church of the New Hebrides, General Assembly Minutes, 1968:27.

25For example, the Solomon Islands Christian Association, in its mimeographed handbook issued in 1983, said that the World Council of Churches would support a Christian education person on its staff and a studio for making broadcasting tapes, but that it was hoped that the recurrent budget would be met by local churches. The wealthiest of these Solomon Island churches, however, received most of its funds from New Zealand. The Fiji Council of Churches announced in 1983 that while it had been subsidized by the World Council in previous years, it was not requesting that subsidy for 1984 in the hope that local churches would provide its support. The Vanuatu Council of Churches in 1983 asked foreign churches to provide $11,000 of its $14,400 budget.

26Norman Healey, A Brief Introduction to the Kiribati Protestant Church, [Tarawa: Church Headquarters, 1983], 12, 7. For Tahiti see Samuel Raapoto, "Eglise Evangelique de Polynesie Francaise," Journal des Missions Evangeliques 149 (1974), no. 4-5, 12-14.

27Hannes Ganszbauer, "Was Kommt Zuruck, "in Theologische Beitrage aus Papua Neuguinea, ed. by Horst Burkle, [Erlangen: Verlag der Ev. Luth. Mission], 1978, 312-313. Brian Turner, "A Nation of Beggars?", 98-99.

[28]Norman Healey, A Brief Introduction to the Kiribati Protestant Church, 12. Francis X. Hezel to author, Oct. 4, 1983. In New Caledonia and Fiji the Catholics have reduced foreign dependence in recent years by the decision of local catechists to serve as volunteers, receiving no pay from the mission or from their congregations. John Snijders, "A Review. Catholic Catechists of the Southwest Pacific," Catalyst, vol. 1, no. 4, 25.

[29]Sione Uesile Tamaali'i, "Church Administration and Finance in the Methodist Church in Samoa," B. D. project, Pacific Theological College, 1975, 95.

[30]The Seventh-Day Adventists came fairly close to being self-supporting in the inner, churchly operations of their work in the Solomons, Tonga and some other islands where they were well established. But usually they were considerably dependent on outside funds for part of their church work and everywhere their important educational and medical services required large funds from abroad. Because they could rely on these funds they did not withdraw from education or medicine or submerge their educational and medical work in the national government systems as the other churches did in the 1970s.

[31]Darrell Whiteman, Melanesians and Missionaries, 153, 384.

BIBLIOGRAPHY

Ahnne, Edward. Dans les Iles du Pacifique. Paris: Societe des Missions Evangeliques, 1931.

Andrew, John. Rebuilding the Christian Commonwealth: New England Congregationalists and Foreign Missions. Lexington: University Press of Kentucky, 1976.

Bach, John. "The Royal Navy in the Pacific Islands." The Journal of Pacific History, 3 (1968):3-20.

Barradale, V. A. Report of Rev. V.A. Barradale after Secretarial Visit to the South Seas, Papua, Australia and New Zealand, August 1926 - June 1927 (with the Rev. G.J. Williams in Papua). London: London Missionary Society, 1927.

Beeching, Jack. An Open Path: Christian Missionaries 1515-1914. London: Hutchinson, 1947.

Bingham, Hiram. A Residence of Twenty-One Years in the Sandwich Islands. Hartford: H. Huntington, 1849.

Boutilier, James. "Missions, Administration and Education in the Solomon Islands, 1893-1942." In Mission, Church, and Sect in Oceania. Edited by James Boutilier et al., 129-161. Ann Arbor: The University of Michigan Press, 1978.

Boyd, Lois A. and R. Douglas Brackenridge. Presbyterian Women In America: Two Centuries of a Quest for Status. Westport: Greenwood Press, 1983.

Brumberg, Joan J. Mission for Life. New York: Free Press, 1980.

_____. "Zenanas and Girless Villages: The Ethnology of American Evangelical Women, 1870-1910." Journal of American History 69(2) (Sep 1982):347-371.

Coan, Mrs. Titus. A Brief Sketch of the Missionary Life of Mrs. Sybil Moseley Bingham. n.p. 1895.

Cott, Nancy F. The Bonds of Womanhood: "Woman's Sphere" in New England, 1780-1835. New Haven: Yale University Press, 1977.

Corris, Peter. Passage, Port and Plantation: A History of
Solomon Islands Labour Migration, 1870-1914. Melbourne:
Melbourne University Press, 1973.

Craig, C. Stuart. "Notes on a Secretarial Visit to Fiji, 16
April-17 May, 1961." Mimeographed. London: London Missionary
Society, 1961.

Davis, Harold. "Auctioneers of Paradise." American Mercury
36 (1935):216-217.

Daws, Gavan. Shoal of Time: A History of the Hawaiian
Islands. New York: MacMillan, 1968.

Deeken, Richard. "Schulinspektor auf Reisen." In Manuia
Samoa. Samoanische Reiseskizzen und Beobachtungen. Berlin
and Oldenburg: Gerhard Stalling, 1901.

Degler, Carl. At Odds: Women and the Family in America from
the Revolution to the Present. New York: Oxford University
Press, 1980.

Dening, Greg. Islands and Beaches: Discourse on a Silent
Land: Marquesas, 1774-1880. Honolulu: The University Press
of Hawaii, 1980.

Dibble, Sheldon. A History of the Sandwich Islands.
Honolulu: T.H. Thrum, 1909.

Forman, Charles W. The Island Churches of the South Pacific.
Emergence in the Twentieth Century. Maryknoll, N.Y.: Orbis
Books, 1982.

Fredrichs, Albert & Sylvia. Anutu Conquers in New Guinea:
The Story of 70 years of Mission Work in New Guinea. Revised
edition. Minneapolis: Augsburg Press, 1969.

Gallaudet, Thomas H. "An Address Delivered at a Meeting for
Prayer." Hartford: Lincoln and Stone, 1819.

Ganszbauer, Hannes. "Was Kommt Zuruck." In Theologische
Beitrage aus Papua Neuguinea. Edited by Horst Burkle,
311-322. Erlangen: Verlag der Ev.-Luth. Mission, 1978.

Garrett, John. "The Conflict Between the London Missionary
Society and the Wesleyan Methodists in Mid-Nineteenth
Century Samoa." The Journal of Pacific History 9 (1974):
65-80.

_____. To Live Among the Stars: Christian Origins in Oceania. Geneva: World Council of Churches, 1982.

Gilson, Richard. The Cook Islands: 1820-1950. Wellington: Victoria University of Wellington, 1980.

Goodall, Norman. Report...after a Secretarial Visit to the Pacific. London: London Missionary Society, 1940.

_____. A History of the London Missionary Society 1895-1945. London: Oxford University Press, 1954.

Gunn, William. The Gospel in Futuna with Chapters on the Islands of the New Hebrides, the People, their Customs, Religious Beliefs, etc. London: Hodder & Stoughton, 1914.

Hanlon, David. "God V. Gods: The First Years of the Micronesian Mission in Ponape, 1852-1859." Unpublished mss., 1983.

Healey, Norman. A Brief Introduction to the Kiribati Protestant Church. Tarawa: Church Headquarters, 1983.

Herbert, T. Walter. Marquesan Encounters: Melville and the Meaning of Civilization. Cambridge: Harvard University Press, 1980.

Hilliard, David. "Colonialism and Christianity: The Melanesian Mission in the Solomon Islands." The Journal of Pacific History 9 (1974):93-116.

_____. God's Gentlemen: A History of the Melanesian Mission, 1849-1942. St. Lucia: University of Queensland Press, 1978.

_____. "Protestant Missions in the Solomon Islands 1849-1942." Ph.D. thesis. Australian National University, 1966.

_____. "The South Sea Evangelical Mission in the Solomon Islands: The Foundation Years." Journal of Pacific History 4 (1969):41-64.

Howe, K. R. Where the Waves Fall. Honolulu: The University of Hawaii Press, 1984.

Humphrey, Herman. "The Promised Land." Boston: Samuel T. Armstrong, 1819.

Kanter, Rossbeth Moss. Work and Family in the United
States: A Critical Review and Agenda for Research and
Policy. New York: Russell Sage Foundation, 1977.

Keesing, Roger. "Christians and Pagans in Kwaio, Malaita."
The Journal of the Polynesian Society 76 (1967):82-100.

Langmore, D. "A Neglected Force: White Women Missionaries
in Papua, 1874-1914." Journal of Pacific History 17(3):
138-157.

Laracy, Hugh. "The Catholic Mission." In Friendly Islands:
A History of Tonga. Edited by Noel Rutherford, 136-153.
Melbourne: Oxford University Press, 1977.

_____. Marists and Melanesians: A History of Catholic
Missions in the Solomon Islands. Honolulu: The University
Press of Hawaii, 1976.

Latukefu, Sione. "The Wesleyan Mission." In Friendly
Islands: A History of Tonga. Edited by Noel Rutherford,
114-135. Melbourne: Oxford University Press, 1977.

_____. "The Impact of South Sea Islands Missionaries on
Melanesia." In Mission, Church, and Sect in Oceania. Edited
by James Boutilier, et al, 91-108. Ann Arbor: The University
of Michigan Press, 1978.

Lebeau, Henri. "Le Christianisme et la musique populaire."
In Otaheiti, au pays de l'éternel été., 227-259. Paris:
Librairie Armand Colin, 1911.

Macdonald, Barrie. Cinderellas of the Empire: Towards a
History of Kiribati and Tuvalu. Canberra: Australian
National University Press, 1982.

Maude, H.E. Of Islands and Men: Studies in Pacific History.
Melbourne: Oxford University Press, 1968.

Methodist Church of Australasia. Report and Recommendations
of the Commission appointed by the Mission Board to Visit
the Fiji District, 1917. Also the Resolution of the Mission
Board. Sydney: Epworth Printing and Publishing House,
1917.

Methodist Church of Australasia. Methodist Missionary
Society: Commission re Native Church 1922. Copy of
Memorandum. Sydney: Printed for Private Circulation. In
Methodist Archives, Sydney, 1923.

Miller, J. Graham. Live. A History of Church Planning in the New Hebrides to 1880. Book One. Sydney: Christian Education Committee, General Assembly of Australia, 1978.

Miller, Char. Fathers and Sons: The Bingham Family and the American Mission. Philadelphia: Temple University Press, 1982.

Neill, Stephen. Colonialism and Christian Missions. New York: McGraw Hill Book Company, 1966.

Newbury, Colin. Tahiti Nui: Change and Survival in French Polynesia 1767-1948. Honolulu: The University Press of Hawaii, 1980.

Nottage, Basil R.C. New Hebrides Calling. Auckland: Presbyterian Church of New Zealand, 1940.

Oosterwal, Gottfried. "Introduction" in Mission, Church, and Sect in Oceania. Edited by James Boutilier, et al., 31-34. Ann Arbor: The University of Michigan Press, 1978

Papanek, Hanna. "Men, Women and Work: Reflections on the Two-Person Career." American Journal of Sociology 17, Summer 1973:852-872.

Raapoto, Samuel. "Eglise Evangélique de Polynesie Francaise." Journal des Missions Evangéliques 149 (1974), no. 4-5:9-15.

Ralston, Caroline. "The Role of the Kamehameha Family in Hawaiian Government." Presented to the 94th American Historical Association Meetings, December 1979.

Ruggles, Samuel and Nancy. "From a Missionary Journal." Atlantic Monthly 134 (November 1924).

Rutherford, Noel. "Shirley Baker and the Kingdom of Tonga." Ph.D. thesis, Australian National University, 1966.

Schloesing, E. "Rapport de M.E. Schloesing sur son Voyage en Océanie (Nov. 1951-Mar. 1952)." Mimeographed. Société des Missions Evangéliques de Paris, 1952.

Silverman, Jane L. "To Marry Again." Hawaiian Journal of History 17, 1983:64-75.

Snijders, John. "A Review. Catholic Catechists of the South-West Pacific, Catalyst 1 (1971), no. 4:21-30.

South Pacific Missionary Conference. The Cross across the
Pacific. Report of Conference of Missionary Leaders Held at
Morpeth, N.S.W. from Feb. 23 to 28, 1948. Sydney: National
Missionary Council of Australia, 1948.

Tamaali'i, Sione Uesile. "Church Administration and Finance
in the Methodist Church in Samoa." B.D. project, Pacific
Theological College, 1975.

Thornley, A.W. "Fijian Methodism 1874-1945. The Emergence
of a National Church." Ph.D. thesis. Australian National
University, 1979.

Threlfall, Neville. One Hundred Years in the Islands. The
Methodist/United Church in the New Guinea Islands Region
1875-1975. Rabaul: United Church, 1975.

Tiffany, Sharon. "Politics of Denominational Organization in
Samoa." In Mission, Church, and Sect in Oceania. Edited by
James Boutilier, et, al., 423-456. Ann Arbor: The University
of Michigan Press, 1978.

Tippett, Alan. People Movements in Southern Polynesia: A
Study in Church Growth. Chicago: Moody Press, 1971.

Turner, Brian. "A Nation of Beggars?" Catalyst 6 (1976),
no. 2:92-101.

Viner, A.J. Willilams, G.J., and Lenwood, Frank. Report
of... Deputation to the South Seas and Papua (with a chapter
on the organization in Australia) June 1915-June 1916.
London: London Missionary Society, 1916.

Webb, M.C. "The Abolition of the Taboo System in Hawaii."
Journal of the Polynesian Society 74(1), March 1965:21-39.

Welter, Barbara. "The Cult of True Womanhood: 1820-1860."
American Quarterly 18 (Summer 1966):151-174.

_____. "She Hath Done What She Could: Protestant
Women's Careers in Nineteenth Century America." American
Quarterly 30 (Winter 1978):624-638.

Whiteman, Darrell. Melanesians and Missionaries, An
Ethnohistorical Study of Social and Religious Change in the
Southwest Pacific. Pasadena: William Carey Library, 1983.

Williams, John. A Narrative of Missionary Enterprises in the
South Sea Islands.... London: John Snow, 1838.

Wiltgen, Ralph. <u>The Founding of the Roman Catholic Church in Oceania, 1825 to 1850</u>. Canberra: Australian National University Press, 1979.